Being an
EFFECTIVE
MENTOR

Second Edition

In loving memory of my father,
Raymond Lloyd Feeney
1921–2002

Master tradesman;
Mentor to scores of apprentices.

Second Edition

Being an EFFECTIVE MENTOR

How to
Help
Beginning
Teachers
Succeed

Kathleen Feeney Jonson

CORWIN PRESS
A SAGE Company
Thousand Oaks, CA 91320

For information:

Corwin Press
A SAGE Company
2455 Teller Road
Thousand Oaks, California 91320
www.corwinpress.com

SAGE Ltd.
1 Oliver's Yard
55 City Road
London EC1Y 1SP
United Kingdom

SAGE India Pvt. Ltd.
B 1/I 1 Mohan Cooperative
   Industrial Area
Mathura Road, New Delhi 110 044
India

SAGE Asia-Pacific Pte. Ltd.
33 Pekin Street #02-01
Far East Square
Singapore 048763

Printed in the United States of America.

Library of Congress Cataloging-in-Publication Data

Jonson, Kathleen Feeney.
Being an effective mentor: how to help beginning teachers succeed/Kathleen Feeney Jonson.—2nd ed.
    p. cm.
Includes bibliographical references and index.
ISBN 978-1-4129-4061-0 (cloth)
ISBN 978-1-4129-4062-7 (pbk.)
    1. Mentoring in education—United States—Handbooks, manuals, etc. 2. First year teachers—Training of—United States—Handbooks, manuals, etc. I. Title.

LB1731.4.J66 2008
371.102—dc22   2007034215

This book is printed on acid-free paper.

08   09   10   11   12   10 9 8 7 6 5 4 3 2 1

Acquisitions Editor:	Dan Alpert
Editorial Assistant:	Tatiana Richards
Production Editor:	Cassandra Margaret Seibel
Copy Editor:	Gail Naron Chalew
Typesetter:	C&M Digitals (P) Ltd.
Proofreader:	Susan Schon
Indexer:	Jean Casalegno
Cover Designer:	Lisa Miller

Contents

Preface to the Second Edition

Has there been anyone in your personal or professional life to whom you've regularly turned for advice and support? Someone who has had a significant and positive impact on your career as an educator? A caring co-worker you might even call your "mentor"?

Many veteran teachers were never actually assigned a mentor. If they were lucky, they found informal assistance from experienced co-workers. Many think back to their first year in the classroom and remember the confusion of a difficult and lonely time when no one came to their aid.

Fortunately, times are changing. Policies to establish teacher mentoring programs are currently sweeping the nation. At this writing, 28 states and the District of Columbia have instituted formal, funded, and mandated mentoring programs. Of course, even today, not all beginning teachers are fortunate enough to get the support they may need, but it is certainly a step in the right direction that someone like you is reading this book.

Mentoring programs attract caring and committed teachers who recognize the complex and challenging nature of classroom teaching. In mentoring, these teachers demonstrate their hope and optimism for the future. They "pass the torch" by helping a new teacher become effective. They hope the beginner will discover the joys and satisfactions that they have found in their own careers. Mentors are not naive Pollyannas, however. They understand that mentoring can be a challenging endeavor requiring significant investments of time and energy. They have lots of empathy, but their decision to help is grounded in the real and the practical.

Mentoring is defined as the professional practice that provides support, assistance, and guidance to beginning teachers to promote their professional growth and success. It is sometimes one program within a larger teacher induction program that also includes other activities such as orientations and inservices. The mentoring component is usually—but not always—a one-on-one relationship. A mentor can serve as a friend, guide, counselor, supporter, and teacher.

In a complex and demanding profession such as teaching, there's no substitute for experience and a repertoire of "tried and true" strategies. Many beginning teachers find the stressful reality of their own classroom to be a shock. They struggle to cope. These new teachers—and their students—deserve the support and guidance of a skilled and experienced mentor.

This book discusses the need for mentoring programs and provides useful strategies for mentors to use to help beginning teachers. Part I, Setting the Stage for the Teacher-Mentor, explains the context for mentoring programs, describes components of a successful program, reminds the teacher-mentor of the experiences and necessary skills of beginning teachers, and positions the mentor in the broader scope of teacher induction programs and professional development. This part not only is useful as context for teacher-mentors but it also provides helpful information for administrators establishing mentor programs in their schools. Part II, Effective Strategies for the Good Mentor, provides a wealth of useful strategies for mentors working with new teachers. Part III, Putting It All Together, offers specific activities for mentors to use with their mentees and provides a checklist as a practical guide.

In Part I, Chapters 1 (Passing the Torch) and 2 (Setup for Success) provide a knowledge base useful to those structuring a mentor program. These introductory chapters contain a historical and policy perspective. In this sense, they are particularly important for staff developers and program administrators as well as for teacher leaders. They provide teachers and administrators with an understanding of the principles and prerequisites of successful mentoring programs. Topics explored include the role of the mentor, qualifications of a good mentor, and the importance of providing preparation and support for the mentoring process. New to this second edition is an expanded discussion of successful programs in Chapter 2, as well as a look at some possible variations in mentor programs.

In Chapter 3, Remembering the First Days, mentors are encouraged to think back on their own first days in the classroom as they prepare to work with new teachers. "Reality shock" and the fears and anxieties of beginners are discussed. Chapter 4, Beyond Survival, provides an overview of the myriad of skills that beginners need to get off to a good start: teaching skills, interpersonal skills, and coping skills. Helping the beginner acquire these skills requires that the mentor perform a variety of functions. These functions range from serving as a role model in the full scope of daily professional activities to developing specific skills such as classroom observation.

An all-new Chapter 5, Moving Toward Professionalism, sets the mentor in the broader context of teacher induction programs. It takes a close look at the Santa Cruz New Teacher Project, one program that is working and serves as a model for other programs. This new chapter also examines ways mentors can help teachers move beyond their initial need to survive and toward professionalism for a successful long-term teaching career. Finally, the chapter outlines some mentoring variations that are particularly useful for the teacher who is no longer a novice.

How mentors develop trusting relationships is the heart of Chapter 6, Working as a Partner With the Adult Learner, the first chapter in Part II. Because mentoring relationships go through phases, Chapter 6 deals with how mentors need to adjust their responses as their protégés develop. Reflection is encouraged as an activity to promote refinement and discovery. Another chapter new to this second edition, Stages in Teacher Development (Chapter 7), explores the stages of development typical for teachers through two models—one that tracks the teacher through the first year on the job and another that looks at development throughout the teaching career.

Chapter 8, Practical Strategies for Assisting New Teachers, explores specific strategies for mentoring. These include direct assistance, demonstration teaching, observation and feedback, informal contact, assistance with an action plan for professional growth, and role modeling. New to the second edition is a section on assessing student work.

And finally, Chapter 9, Overcoming Obstacles and Reaping the Rewards, takes a close look at the pitfalls and payoffs of mentoring. The chapter includes an expanded discussion of ways for mentors to deal with some pitfalls, notably finding time to mentor in addition to all of the other teacher tasks and how to work with difficult mentees. The chapter also looks at the important question, Why be a mentor? There is little doubt that ongoing, meaningful contact between mentors and protégés reinforces and fosters professional development and builds trust—and the benefits are for mentors as well as for their mentees.

In Part III, Putting It All Together, the mentor finds a month-by-month listing of suggested activities designed to promote interaction between mentors and their protégés. Activities have been suggested for each month to correspond with activities and events typically occurring in a school year. Following the monthly list of activities is a checklist for mentors to use as a practical guide. Finally, three appendixes provide valuable information and tools to help the mentor work with the beginning teacher.

Although intended primarily for mentors, this book will be of interest to anyone concerned with the complex process of guidance, assistance, and support to promote growth and success for beginning teachers. Principals, staff developers, university supervisors, beginning and experienced teachers, and even parents and community members—we all can benefit from an understanding of the value and process of mentoring.

Acknowledgments

The contributions of the following reviewers for this book are gratefully acknowledged:

Patricia Schwartz
Principal
Thomas Jefferson Middle School
Teaneck, New Jersey

Joan Roberts
Coordinator/Administrator
Monterey County Office of Education
Salinas, California

RoseAnne O'Brien Vojtek
Principal
Ivy Drive Elementary School
Bristol Public Schools
Bristol, Connecticut

Linda Munger
Educational Consultant
Munger Education Associates
Des Moines, Iowa

Marti Richardson
NSDC Board of Trustees
Staff Development Supervisor
Knoxville, Tennessee

Also gratefully acknowledged are the contributions of reviewers for the second edition:

Carol Pelletier
Director, Professional Practice and Induction
Massachusetts

Dr. Tom Ganser
Director, Office of Field Experiences
Wisconsin

Kathy Rosebrock
BTSA Coordinator
California

Hal Portner
Corwin Press Author
Massachusetts

Barry Sweeny
Corwin Press Author
Illinois

About the Author

Kathleen Feeney Jonson, EdD, is currently Professor and Director of the Master of Arts in the Teaching Reading program in the Teacher Education Department of the University of San Francisco. As the oldest of nine children, she says she was born to teach and mentor. In her 37 years as an educator, she has taught at the elementary and secondary levels and has served as a reading specialist, director of staff development, principal, and director of curriculum and instruction. She has conducted numerous workshops for teachers and administrators on such topics as integrating the curriculum, reading comprehension strategies, the writing process, portfolio assessment, peer coaching, and beginning teacher assistance programs. She has developed numerous curriculum guides, training syllabi, and program materials for educators and parents. Her professional experience includes teaching university courses in elementary and secondary curriculum and instruction, as well as serving as Field Coordinator working with student teachers, teacher-mentors, and university supervisors. She has published three books with Corwin Press, including *60 Strategies for Improving Reading Comprehension in Grades K–8* (2006), *The New Elementary Teacher's Handbook*, 2nd ed. (2001), and *Being an Effective Mentor: How to Help Beginning Teachers Succeed*, 1st ed. (2002).

PART I

*Setting the Stage for
the Teacher-Mentor*

1

Passing the Torch

Those having torches will pass them on to others.

—Plato, *The Republic*

Twenty second graders stand in line inside the door to Room 3D at Lincoln Elementary School. "Kyle cut!" Cameron insists, gripping his folder and lunch box. Ms. Blackwell glances at the boys, but Kyle denies the accusation. The clock ticks to 2:40 p.m., and the bell rings. With a weary smile, Ms. Blackwell waves good-bye and watches as the children scurry out, the two boys still arguing. Feeling a sense of relief, she turns back into the classroom. Too late, she discovers that Caitlin has forgotten to put her chair up on her table again, and Danny hasn't picked up his pencil from the floor as she asked him to do. She must work on better follow-through.

Ms. Blackwell kneels to pick up Danny's pencil, lifts up Caitlin's chair, and returns to her desk. Sighing, she looks at the pile of spelling papers on her desk, the large, dark letters carefully—or not so carefully—printed on wide lines. With a glance, she can tell that most of the words on the top paper are misspelled. She had been so sure that her new study-in-buddies idea would work, but apparently it hadn't. At least not for everyone.

Ms. Blackwell sets aside the papers, too disheartened to review them. Her eyes burn as she reflects on her day. Again today, Maggie complained that James was chasing her on the playground. The experiment Ms. Blackwell had planned for the unit on rocks was too difficult. And her throat is burning—but she can't take time off and leave her class with a substitute. She looks at her desk. Oh, and there's that form she was supposed to have returned to the office yesterday. She should take care of that now—except that she doesn't really understand it. Besides, she needs to get to a teachers' meeting by 3:00. She was late to the last one. Better be on time for this one. Don't want to appear unable to manage.

Ms. Blackwell plants the late form in the middle of her desk so she will be sure to see it first thing when she returns, gathers her papers for the meeting, grabs a tissue for her runny nose, and heads out into the hall. She wonders if any of the other new teachers have these problems or if it's just her.

She had done so well at the university, had loved student teaching with Mr. Beverly. What had happened? Would it ever get easier? She had worked so hard last August to set up her classroom perfectly, tacking up colorful wall coverings and organizing things as discussed in her university classes. Everyone—her professors and friends and the people at Mr. Beverly's school—had assured her that she would make a great teacher. But she doesn't seem to be doing so well now. She tries to think about how Mr. Beverly might handle James. But the boys in Mr. Beverly's fourth grade hadn't chased the girls. Seems that few of the problems she faces now came up when she student-taught with Mr. Beverly. If only she had a Mr. Beverly to turn to now.

The anxieties and frustrations that Ms. Blackwell feels are typical of first-year teachers—and sometimes of teachers in general. No matter how well prepared a beginning teacher may be on entering the profession—no matter how positive her preservice experience—the early years are always difficult. Issues of classroom and time management commonly cause significant stress. The tasks to be completed seem endless, and when a problem arises, the teacher, alone in the classroom, cannot turn to a coworker for immediate support as another professional in another field might do. Too often during their first years of on-the-job training, teachers throughout history have had to master their craft by trial and error, in an isolated environment, with little feedback.

The first two years of teaching are particularly critical. During this time, the teacher builds the foundation for what could be a satisfying and productive career. But these first two years are also considered by many to be the hardest. In this profession, unlike in others, the beginning teacher has the same workload and responsibilities as the veteran. Teachers are expected to be experts ready to tackle the biggest challenges on the first day they enter a school (Alliance for Excellent Education, 2004, p. 2). There is no period for adjustment. What might seem to be the simple mechanics of running a real-world classroom from day to day prove to be surprisingly distressing and stressful.

The result? Often during this "induction" period, beginning teachers become frustrated and eager to leave. Far too many report lying awake, unable to sleep at night, fretting about their students and school responsibilities. According to a survey of stress in various professions, teachers (followed by nurses, accountants, and newspaper reporters) are the people most likely to report losing sleep over work-related worries ("Losing Sleep," 2001). This beginning teacher sheds some light on the problem:

> Stress! You're teaching classes all day long. You're keeping students on task, you're testing, you're trying to follow all the rules—every principle and guideline that's set out for you. You're adhering to a schedule: you must teach all the things in the course of study by the end of the year. After school you go home and take your job with you. Then you must face kids who have homework and a husband who has had a tough day, too (quoted in Gordon & Maxey, 2000, p. 66).

To many in their first year of teaching, then, figuring out how to control students whose first instincts are anything but cooperative makes just surviving a real accomplishment. Without assistance and support, these beginning teachers burn out early at a high rate. Some, overwhelmed by all the "juggling" they have to do, leave the teaching profession altogether. Nationwide, 30% of beginning teachers leave the profession within two years, another 10% leave after three years, and more than half leave within five to seven years (Alliance for Excellent Education, 2004, p. 1; Ingersoll, 2001, p. 514; Pearson & Honig, 1992, p. 5). In urban districts, attrition occurs even faster: Half the new teachers are gone within three years (Haberman, 1987; Zimpher & Grossman, 1992, p. 141). According to the Alliance for Excellent Education (2004), the current "rate of attrition among beginning teachers is astronomical."

And this rate of attrition affects everyone: the community that must continue to recruit and train new teachers, the teachers who find themselves leaving a career they had spent years preparing for, and the children. The National Commission on Teaching and America's Future (NCTAF) has gathered information on teacher preparation since the early 1990s and has published many reports on the relationship between teacher quality and student success. In a 2003 report, *No Dream Denied: A Pledge to America's School Children,* the commission states,

> Schools pay a price as high turnover rates force an annual scramble to replace those who leave. Teachers pay a price as their frustrations lead to short-circuited careers. But students pay the highest prices of all: diminished learning and dreams denied (p. 11).

Particularly disturbing is research indicating that the most academically proficient teachers are also the ones who are most likely to leave the field (Schlechty & Vance, 1983; Smith, 1993, p. 6). In a study of beginning teachers in San Diego County, California, a teacher leaving the profession after her first year had received one of only six National Education Outstanding Student Teacher Awards (Mathison, 1996, p. 15). The loss of such a potentially exceptional teacher clearly indicates that something is wrong. And according to First Lady Laura Bush's *Ready to Read, Ready to Learn* initiative, "teachers with higher standardized test scores leave teaching at much higher rates than those with lower scores" (2001, p. 11).

Why would someone who had spent four to six years preparing for a profession leave the career within a year or two? What is it that makes beginning teacher after beginning teacher feel as if his years of study have left him unprepared for the world of teaching? And how can this situation be changed to benefit the children in U.S. classrooms?

ENTER THE MENTOR

Throughout the United States, educational systems began to realize in the early 1980s that a serious problem existed: Teachers need assistance and guidance, especially during their early years in the profession. According to *No Dream Denied*, teacher retention relates strongly not only to adequate preparation (background in subject matter and teaching methods) but also to meaningful induction and mentoring programs (NCTAF, 2003). No matter how well prepared, a teacher such as Ms. Blackwell needs someone to turn to with the inevitable questions and problems that arise as she begins her profession in the classroom.

With this recognition, more than 30 states now mandate support for beginning teachers as part of their teacher induction programs (Portner, 1998, p. 3). Increasingly, school districts are arranging for experienced teachers (*mentors*) to guide beginning teachers (*mentees* or *protégés*) through the difficult early years and to help them develop as professionals. And although this book focuses on support for beginning teachers, it is important to note that teachers new to a system also often need assistance (Smith, 1993, p. 7). In some locations, mentors have been recruited to work not only with beginning teachers but also with teachers new to the district or even with experienced teachers having difficulty. Both of the two latter groups of teachers need practical assistance with tasks such as making schedules for breaks and for lunch, hall, and yard duties, and they need information about where to get supplies and materials, about required forms and meetings, and so on. Like newcomers to the profession, veterans moving to a different location need a realistic view of their new school to help them "understand the challenges that inevitably surface when people experience the transition from one job to another" (Gordon & Maxey, 2000, p. 84). Mentors can help the newcomer understand the culture and philosophy of the school and can provide the emotional and intellectual support needed in the early days and months of adjustment.

The idea of a mentor helping a beginner is nothing new. The term *mentor* itself dates back to the eighth or ninth century BCE, specifically to Homer's *Odyssey*. In his epic poem, Homer describes his hero, Odysseus, as Odysseus prepares to set out on a 10-year voyage. Odysseus must leave behind his son, Telemachus, and asks his trusted friend Mentor to guide and counsel Telemachus in his absence. While the father is gone, Mentor serves as a sage adviser to the younger man, helping him grow intellectually, emotionally, and socially. From this ancient literary figure, *mentor* has come to refer to a wise and faithful counselor who helps guide a protégé through a developmental process. This could be the process of transition from youth to adulthood, as in the case of Telemachus, or from student to professional, as with a first-year teacher.

Modern-day mentors are found in many segments of society. The Big Brother and Big Sister programs are based on the mentor concept: Responsible adults are paired with children; they build a trusting relationship with those children and share with them a variety of activities, guiding them as they grow into young adults. Athletic or drama coaches could also be considered mentors, directing novices in their field. In the professional arena, doctors and lawyers have long been mentored through internship programs, and plumbers, printers, and other skilled tradespeople serve in apprenticeships, another variation of mentorships.

As these examples illustrate, the skills involved, age groups, and degree of formality vary widely among mentoring programs. The common thread, though, is that all such programs are based on a trusting relationship between an experienced adult and a novice. In each case, the organization or business that wants to retain and develop its members provides some sort of mentor support. The idea is not for the mentor to evaluate or judge the protégé, but rather for the mentee to receive guidance. The mentor is defined more by the relationship with a beginner than by a position or title.

Some such relationships happen spontaneously. For example, a new employee asks advice of a more experienced colleague, who sees potential in the beginner and continues to offer support. Other pairings result from a considered design. Large corporations, for example, sometimes match senior managers to ambitious, talented junior employees. Mentors in this situation may help newer employees with such issues as balancing personal and business lives, as well as working within the corporate environment. The mentees learn that their concerns are not unique—that other employees have experienced the same problems—and this knowledge helps them grow professionally.

According to several studies, mentors have played an important role in the career development of many highly successful people in business. In one study, researchers found that businesspeople who had mentors earned more money at a younger age and were more satisfied with their work and career advancement than were those without mentors (Bolton, 1980; Odell,

1990, p. 5; Roche, 1979). Mentoring programs in business were found to help the protégé with personal adjustment, satisfaction, and professional achievement (Bova, 1987; Cohen, 1995, p. 4; Kram, 1985; Marsick, 1987; Zey, 1984). In both university and business settings, protégés of mentors learned risk-taking behaviors, communication skills, political skills, and specific skills that helped them in their professions (Bova & Phillips, 1983; Odell, 1990, p. 6). Even in government, mentors have helped employees develop their careers and prepare for senior positions (Cohen, 1995, p. 4; Murray, 1991).

Mentoring would seem to be a natural progression in the teaching profession, too, where experienced teachers have traditionally passed on their expertise and wisdom to new colleagues. For a beginning teacher, the benefits of working closely with a mentor are great, no matter how extensive the preservice education. Beginning teachers are faced by and accountable for (or to—it is not always clear which) an array of unknown students, teaching colleagues, administrators, and parents. As Ms. Blackwell discovered, even routine paperwork can be overwhelming when the teacher does not understand it and does not know where to look for help. In addition, school and community environments have norms and rituals that are probably new and obscure to a newcomer. The large number of actual and procedural unknowns can send the beginning teacher into a state of shock wherein it becomes impossible to transfer previously mastered concepts and skills from the university to the K–12 classroom. Ms. Blackwell could have benefited greatly from the help of a veteran teacher familiar with her grade level and school site.

So far in education, relatively little hard research has been conducted on the effects of mentoring. Many descriptive studies and program evaluations clearly conclude, however, that a good mentor-mentee relationship significantly benefits the beginning teacher, not only during the difficult first year but also in years to come. Through an examination of the literature and many research studies on beginning teachers, Varah, Theune, and Parker (1986) have concluded that "collaborative teacher induction programs are effective means of strengthening beginning teacher performance" (quoted in Smith, 1993, p. 6). Other studies have also indicated that mentors and induction programs are overwhelmingly successful, increasing the retention of beginning teachers and ameliorating first-year difficulties (Bey, 1992, p. 114; Smith, 1993).

Despite this seemingly natural form of assistance, teachers have had no formal system like those used in businesses through which to receive guidance once they entered their first professional classroom—until recently. Not until the early 1980s did those in the teaching profession begin to take up the mentoring torch. Now the trend is gaining momentum, however. In 1997, the U.S. Secretary of Education included in his initiatives, published in *The Seven Priorities of the U.S. Department of Education,* "special efforts to retain beginning teachers in their first few years of teaching"

(U.S. Department of Education, 1997). That same year, in his *Call to Action for American Education in the 21st Century,* then-President Bill Clinton announced that school districts must "make sure that beginning teachers get support and mentoring from experienced teachers" ("President Clinton's Call," 1997).

With rising student enrollment, teacher attrition ranging from 35% to 50% nationwide during the first five years, class size reduction in some states, and many teachers approaching retirement, the need for new teachers continues. The U.S. Department of Education projected that more than two million new teachers would be needed within the first decade of the twenty-first century (Moir & Gless, n.d., p. 1). Although President George W. Bush has focused more recently on standards and testing, it is increasingly important to guide and retain those who enter the profession if children in the classrooms are to learn.

Teachers themselves support the idea of teacher-mentors. Teachers have reported that they get their best innovative ideas regarding teaching from other teachers (Sergiovanni, 1992, p. 86). In one large national study funded by Public Agenda, many administrators and new teachers expressed a belief that mentoring programs could significantly improve teacher quality (Farkas, Johnson, & Foleno, 2000, p. 29). In another national sample, this one looking at 1,007 beginning teachers, 46% said an experienced teacher assigned to advise and assist them would have been most helpful in preparing them to become more effective as first-year teachers (Bey, 1992, p. 111; Lou Harris & Associates, 1991).

THE ROLE OF THE TEACHER-MENTOR

In the field of teaching, the mentor plays a vital and unique role in the development and training of someone new to the profession. An effective mentor provides support and collegiality, alleviating the isolation so often experienced by the beginning teacher. What makes mentors different from others who may help is that they develop a relationship of trust with beginning teachers over an extended period of time and remain with the mentees as they evolve and as issues develop. One California mentor notes that this trust is particularly important: "My mentee and I have a trusting relationship in that he can be open and honest with his needs." In contrast, a principal, for example, may be available to help with a specific, one-time problem on a practical level, but does not necessarily provide ongoing, daily help with a range of emotional, curricular, and instructional questions.

For a variety of reasons, an experienced colleague is particularly suited to the mentor role. According to Acheson and Gall, "The most available source of expertise is teachers themselves: to analyze their own teaching on the basis of objective data, to observe others' classrooms and record data teachers cannot record themselves, to help one another analyze these data and make decisions about alternative strategies" (as quoted in Heller, 2004, p. 194).

A colleague who is close at hand is available when the mentee needs guidance, in both formal and informal contexts. If both parties work in the same setting and with similar goals, they can often relate to each other's experiences; Ms. Blackwell, for example, might have found help from a mentor who had shared her problems with the students at her school. Because integrity and trust are vital to a good mentor-mentee relationship, many experienced mentors feel strongly that mentors should not be involved in evaluating their mentees. If this is the case, mentees are more likely to share experiences, fears, and concerns without the anxiety of being judged. Those same beginning teachers might be reluctant to share these feelings or problems with their principal, for example, who will later evaluate them and help make decisions about the future of their careers.

The primary task of the mentor, then, is to establish a relationship with the beginning teacher based on mutual trust, respect, and collegiality. Through the sharing of frustrations and successes, the beginning teacher learns that problems are normal, and this helps build confidence. One California mentor believes that important contributions for a mentee might include "validating the challenges of teaching; taking [the mentees'] ideas and feelings seriously; helping them to trust their own judgment." Another points out the value of "discussing problems realistically and letting them know I have the same problems sometimes; just letting them vent."

Support and encouragement from an effective mentor can thus greatly benefit the beginning teacher: In most beginner assistance programs, however, the mentor also directly assists beginning teachers, helping them learn quickly as they are immersed in the complex art and science of teaching. "When I first visited my mentee," one California mentor recalls, "his classroom was completely out of control. Afterward I gave him feedback and five simple, concrete policy suggestions. Immediate implementation led to immediate results." Yet another mentor tells about helping with a specific lesson. "My mentee was having trouble organizing a weather unit," this one said. "So we took a couple of hours and we went through my whole weather file and we made a schedule and lesson plan for the new unit."

Among the mentor's goals, then, should be to help beginning teachers develop and enhance the following attributes:

- Competence: mastery of the knowledge, skills, and applications that effective teaching requires
- Self-confidence: belief in one's ability to make good decisions, to be responsible, and to be in control
- Self-direction: the assurance and ability to take charge of one's personal, professional, and career development

- Professionalism: an understanding and assumption of the responsibilities and ethics of the profession

THE GOOD MENTOR: WHAT DOES IT TAKE?

The task of mentoring is complex and requires the skills of a teacher, counselor, friend, role model, guide, sponsor, coach, resource, and colleague. Through the years, mentors have also gone by the names of *host, supporter, adviser, positive role model, confidant, guru, master teacher, teacher adviser, teacher specialist, colleague teacher, peer teacher,* and *support teacher.*

Under any name, though, the idea is the same: An experienced and expert professional develops a relationship with a trained but inexperienced protégé. The mentor may incorporate a variety of strategies and activities to help the protégé grow and develop in professional competence, attitudes, and behaviors—but regardless of the specific activities and goals, the qualitative nature of the relationship determines the overall effectiveness of the mentor.

So what makes a good mentor? Is it just a matter of being a highly accomplished teacher? Certainly that's a good starting point, but it's not enough. Commitment to promoting excellence in the teaching profession? That's important, too. But even more is required. Mentors are special people. Good ones have qualities and responsibilities that include but go beyond those of a good teacher. For teachers, a good mentor

- is a skilled teacher,
- has a thorough command of the curriculum being taught,
- is able to transmit effective teaching strategies,
- can communicate openly and effectively with the beginning teacher,
- is a good listener,
- is able to transmit effective teaching strategies,
- has strong interpersonal skills,
- has credibility with peers and administrators,
- is sensitive to the needs of the beginning teacher,
- understands that teachers may be effective using a variety of styles,
- is not overly judgmental,
- demonstrates an eagerness to learn, and
- demonstrates a commitment to improving the academic achievement of all students.

Studies show that other desirable qualities in a mentor include wisdom, caring, humor, nurturing, and commitment to the profession (Hardcastle, 1988; Kay, 1990; Odell, 1990, p. 11). If the job were to be posted, an announcement might read something like that in Box 1.1.

BOX 1.1

Job Announcement

Teacher-Mentor

Description

Experienced teachers who have mastered their craft and who are dedicated to promoting excellence in the teaching profession are sought as mentors for beginning teachers just starting their careers. Mentors must play several roles, including guide, role model, sponsor, counselor, coach, resource, and colleague.

Responsibilities

As a mentor, you will be responsible for

- Meeting regularly with your protégé, both formally and informally
- Guiding your protégé through the daily operation of the school
- Arranging for your protégé to visit different teachers' classes
- Demonstrating lessons for your protégé
- Observing your protégé's teaching and providing feedback
- Being a role model in all aspects of professionalism
- Developing your skills as a mentor as well as a teacher
- Supporting and counseling your protégé, providing perspective when needed

Qualifications

It takes a special person to be a good mentor. Maturity, self-assurance, patience, and confidence in your knowledge and ability are prerequisites for this important undertaking. More specifically, a good mentor is a teacher who

- Is a skillful teacher
- Is able to transmit effective teaching strategies
- Has a thorough command of the curriculum being taught
- Is a good listener
- Can communicate openly with the beginning teacher
- Is sensitive to the needs of the beginning teacher
- Understands that teachers may be effective using a variety of styles
- Is careful not to be overly judgmental

Conditions of Employment

Extra time, effort, and commitment are required. Increased contact with colleagues, professional stimulation, and sense of accomplishment are likely. Tangible compensation—never enough; intangible rewards—priceless.
   Mentors needed every year! Apply now!

Requirements for mentoring go even beyond these general characteristics and qualities. Good mentors understand the needs of beginning teachers and of teachers building professionalism (Chapters 3 through 5).

They are armed with effective instructional coaching strategies appropriate for the adult learner (Chapters 6 and 7). Problem-solving skills and the ability to think critically and reflectively are also prerequisites.

Mentoring requires commitment and a willingness to extend oneself for another person. Good mentors must be conscious that their own professional development serves as a model for the beginning teacher and that lifelong learning is as much an attitude as it is an activity; for true professionals, learning is a way of life. With an effective program, the rewards include not only the satisfaction of helping a beginning teacher succeed but also personal and professional growth for the mentor.

> Being a mentor keeps me current. When I have to answer my mentee's questions, it makes me ask, "Why am I doing what I'm doing?" In discussing philosophy, problems, or techniques with this new teacher, I find out what I really believe. That makes me a stronger person and a better teacher.
>
> —A mentor (quoted in Gordon & Maxey, 2000, p. 66)

CONCLUSION

This book provides the rationale and guidelines for setting up an effective mentoring program as well as practical information and advice for new mentors. Chapter 1 opened Part I, Setting the Stage for the Teacher-Mentor, explaining to mentors why their role is important; this information is also useful for those developing mentoring programs. The mentor plays an especially important role in helping the beginning teacher adjust to a new profession, but a mentor can also be of assistance to a veteran teacher new to a particular setting. In the next chapter, I review several successful programs and discuss their common elements.

The following chapters give guidance for mentors in their new roles, reminding them what it was like to be a beginning teacher (Chapter 3) and what basic skills are required of every teacher (Chapter 4). Chapter 5 gives more contextual information about induction programs and how mentors fit into those programs; it discusses variations on mentoring that are particularly useful in helping the teacher progress toward professionalism.

Part II of the book, Effective Strategies for the Good Mentor, opens with Chapter 6 and a discussion of general aspects of working with adult learners; Chapter 7 then talks about stages of development of teachers in particular. Chapter 8 gives concrete strategies for working with beginning teachers. Finally, Chapter 9 discusses typical challenges faced by mentors, including finding time for the endeavor and dealing with difficult mentees—but then answers the question, Why be a mentor anyway?

Part III, Putting It All Together, includes practical aids for approaching the challenge of helping a beginning teacher adjust to a difficult but rewarding career.

If teaching is ever to be a profession in the sense that medicine and law are, beginning teachers need a chance to learn what constitutes good practice with the help of accomplished colleagues instead of being forced to figure everything out for themselves (Shanker, 1995).

2

Setup for Success

Dolores sits before a group of young children in her elementary school class-room. Until recently, she worked as an executive for a large corporation. Now she is making the transition to a new profession.

Nancy, a veteran teacher, is in the back of the classroom taking notes as Dolores engages her young students in a round of the song, "Wheels on the Bus." Later, the children remain attentive as their teacher reads aloud to them from a picture book.

After the children leave, Nancy and Dolores sit together at a table in the classroom to discuss the events of the day. Nancy points out that the children were involved in the movements of the opening song and suggests that Dolores help them create movements to go along with the pages of the book as well. She comments on the beginning teacher's method for getting attention (a hand signal using a countdown on fingers) and says with enthusiasm that she plans to try the method in her own classroom the next day.

The two teachers laugh at times as they converse, comfortable with each other, sharing ideas. The mood is friendly and receptive, and it is clear that even two good teachers—both the mentor and the mentee—can become stronger teachers through their relationship.

—Summary of the video, *Mentoring to Improve Schools*

(ASCD, 1999b)

In this scenario, Dolores and Nancy work well together in a program that has been set up to support mentors and mentees. Nancy has the qualities of a good mentor—experience as a teacher herself, openness to Dolores's teaching style, and good interpersonal skills, among other things—and Dolores is eager to grow as a professional. Dolores and Nancy also benefit from working in an established program with supports in place for both the mentor and mentee. Their district in Fairfax County, Virginia, is only one of many throughout the United States that have implemented mentoring programs for their beginning teachers during the past two-and-a-half decades. Individual programs vary in the details of how they are set up, but all have been established to help beginning teachers survive the initial shock of teaching reality and progress to become quality educators.

Following are examples of seven successful programs. After describing these programs, the chapter discusses their common elements and variations. This chapter then looks at the prerequisite qualifications most likely to lead to successful mentors, followed by a discussion of program elements for success. It concludes with a description of some variations on mentor programs.

EXEMPLARY PROGRAMS ACROSS THE UNITED STATES

Fairfax County, Virginia. In the Virginia county where Dolores and Nancy teach, every beginning teacher or teacher new to a school automatically participates in a three-year program that pairs the beginning teacher with a veteran teacher. These veteran teachers, or mentors, work with the assistance of a program coordinator—a sort of mentor's mentor—who does everything from helping pair the mentor with mentees to coaching mentors to providing other types of support. The idea is that the veteran teacher will help the novice learn about the school environment and philosophy, become familiar with the curriculum, and understand district procedures and goals. In the scenario at the beginning of this chapter, for example, Nancy helped Dolores with her curriculum.

Ultimately, the goals in the Fairfax program are to (a) improve teaching, (b) enhance administrative practices, and (c) create a learning community. In the first year of the program, the focus is on helping the beginning teacher survive. In the second year, mentors help the beginning teachers reflect on their own work. By the third year, the beginning teachers suggest topics that they are concerned about and would like to work on.

In addition to working with a mentor, beginning teachers in Fairfax County attend weekly meetings where they work on their teaching skills and gain additional support. One week, the meetings are geared to teach the participants, and they include only beginning and new teachers. Alternating weeks, the meetings are geared for reflection on the previous week's discussion and are open to experienced teachers as well. As the teachers work together, they become stronger and better able to help the children.

Minneapolis, Minnesota. The school system of Minneapolis, Minnesota, uses a different variation on the mentor process (ASCD, 1999b). There, too, beginning teachers work with mentors over a three-year period. However, in Minneapolis, the experienced teacher serves as a full-time mentor, relieved of all other teaching responsibilities for the period of the mentorship. Teachers in the system like this program model because it allows them to develop their mentoring relationships and spend more time in their mentor-mentee pairs.

In the Minneapolis system, unlike in many others, the mentor takes part in evaluating the beginning teacher and in making the decision whether to retain the teacher—but only after the third year. Although most experts agree that mentors should *not* be involved in evaluating their protégés, mentors in this district say it works in their case and may be a fairer way of evaluating a beginning teacher than having an assessment performed by another individual who doesn't have the time required to fully understand a situation.

Kentucky. In 1985, Kentucky mandated the formation of the Kentucky Teacher Internship Program. In this program, a collegial team helps induct all beginning teaching professionals within the state (Brennan, Thames, & Roberts, 1999, p. 49). The program includes conferences, committee meetings, and 50 hours of paid mentor time with the mentee. New teachers receive structured assistance and assessment from a committee that includes not only a mentor-teacher but also a university representative and the school principal. Committee members use observations and portfolios to assess the beginning teacher's professional progress. During the first two years of a teacher's induction, assessment is formative, or advisory. During the third year, it is used as a basis for permanent certification.

California. In California, beginning teachers are supported and encouraged through the Beginning Teacher Support and Assessment (BTSA) program, funded by the state since 1992. BTSA began as the California New Teacher Project, a research program conducted from 1988 to 1992 that examined alternative strategies for supporting and assessing beginning teachers. The program was established to provide new teachers with high-quality professional development based on the California Standards for the Teaching Profession and with support from experienced teachers. It involves on-site coaching, meetings of beginning teachers with support providers, grade-level support seminars, release time for professional growth, funds for supplies, field-based coursework, access to district professional development programs, and training of administrators. BTSA has become a hugely successful program and serves as a model for programs being developed in other states. In this program, as in many others, the mentor is only one vital component in a larger induction program set up to help teachers begin their professional careers. Annual retention surveys by the California Commission on Teacher Credentialing indicate that 84% of the teachers who participated in BTSA programs remained in teaching five years later (California Department of Education, 2006, p. 8). For more about induction programs, see Chapter 5, Moving Toward Professionalism.

School districts within the state of California have set up programs under BTSA in different ways. In the San Francisco Unified School District, the program involves not only the school district but also the teacher education departments of local universities. The idea is to bridge the knowledge and skills from preservice education to on-the-job experience.

In San Francisco, a school district mentor, or support provider, is assigned to each beginning teacher. The mentor assists and guides beginning teachers but does not evaluate them. One second-year teacher who benefited from the program her second year, but not her first, wrote in her journal,

> Last year I had no support system or extra help in coping with the immense problems and little everyday things that happen. I felt alone. I learned to cope by myself. I worked 14 hours a day. This year . . . I have a network of people to call on for help or ideas. I can hardly believe what a positive influence the communication has had on my life. I don't have to reinvent the wheel anymore.

Participants asked to assess their experiences with the project especially and repeatedly lauded the mentoring support they received (Jonson, 1998, pp. 23–24).

Connecticut. Through Connecticut's Beginning Educator Support and Training (BEST) program, new teachers receive support as a group through school- or district-based mentors or support teams. To ensure consistency of support throughout the state, BEST requires that all school-based mentoring programs adhere to the following standards:

- Mentors are selected by a district committee consisting of teachers and administrators.
- Mentor or mentor teams are assigned to work with beginning teachers for a minimum of one year, with regular meetings.

- Beginning teachers are provided with release time on at least eight occasions to observe or be observed by their mentors or members of the support team.
- Accomplished teachers appointed as mentors receive a minimum of 20 hours of initial training in Connecticut's teaching standards, the portfolio assessment process, and coaching strategies.

Mentors and beginning teachers in Connecticut typically spend time together exploring teaching strategies that address diversity in students and their learning styles, identifying effective teaching strategies that conform to state standards, and reflecting on the progress of the new teacher's students. Teachers appointed as mentors enroll in a mentoring course at one of the regional educational service centers, where they learn coaching strategies and develop their skills. Mentors find support within a network of peers at their mentoring course as they work with new teachers. Their training also includes an overview of the portfolio assessment process and strategies to assist teachers in demonstrating their mastery of Connecticut's teaching standards. Each summer, more than 600 exemplary teachers and administrators get together to score the portfolios and to determine whether the mentee teachers are qualified to continue in the profession (Alliance for Excellent Education, 2004).

Tangipahoa Parish, Louisiana. In Louisiana, the Department of Education administers two statewide programs to systematically support and develop new teachers: the Louisiana Teacher Assistance and Assessment Program (LaTAAP) and the Louisiana Framework for Inducting, Retaining, and Supporting Teachers (LaFIRST). LaTAAP specifies qualifications for mentors, who must train with a local state-trained instructor. Mentor activities include weekly meetings with new teachers and classroom observations. Each LaTAAP mentor supports only one or two novices, ensuring time to assist each. Most new teachers spend an average of one to two hours per week with their mentor. Under this program, principals must schedule time for mentors to work with teachers and monitor their activities, and mentors and new teachers must have common planning time. In Tangipahoa Parish, FIRST provides four full-time trained mentors and four half-time trained mentors to supplement the work of LaTAAP mentors by assisting new teachers, including special education teachers. These mentors receive LaTAAP Assessor and Mentor Trainings, Tangipahoa FIRST mentor training, and monthly follow-up training by the program coordinator. Because FIRST mentors do not have classes of their own, they can help overwhelmed teachers research activities, develop lesson plans, gather materials, and grade papers.

"Having a mentor teacher has been the most helpful learning experience for me as a teacher," one Tangipahoa new teacher commented. "At all times, I was able to ask questions, see models, and hear related experiences. This has helped me to develop my teaching skill and grow as a professional"

(Alliance for Excellent Education, 2004). Three Tangipahoa teachers participating in a focus group about their experiences noted that the help of the full-time mentors kept them from leaving their jobs. These teachers credited the mentors for building their confidence, helping them improve their teaching ability, and causing them to look forward to coming back for another year in the classroom.

Toledo, Ohio. Under the Toledo Plan, teachers apply to become a mentor, or intern consultant, by filling out an application, obtaining letters of reference from their school principal, agreeing to two unannounced observations of their classroom teaching, submitting a writing sample, and completing an interview. Candidates must be licensed in their subject area, and most have more than five years of teaching experience. After the Board of Review selects the applicants to be hired, new consultants train by observing and working with veterans and participating in a two- to three-day summer training workshop. Intern consultants are released full-time from their classroom responsibilities for a three-year period while they mentor and evaluate.

At the beginning of the school year, new teachers in the Toledo Plan are paid to attend a mandatory five-day New Teacher Academy. At this academy, new teachers meet their intern consultants and receive an orientation to teaching resources and district policies. Later, during the school year, mentors spend much of their time making classroom observations and having individual conferences, giving roughly 20 hours per semester to mentor and evaluate each of 10 to 12 interns. Consultants observe each new teacher in the classroom two to three times a month and then meet with the new teacher to discuss strengths and areas for growth, with the goals of improving instruction and classroom management.

The Toledo Plan is designed to ensure that quality teachers return to their classrooms. After three years, the intern consultants go back to their classrooms to teach (Alliance for Excellent Education, 2004).

Similarities and Differences. Although each of the preceding examples has similarities with the others, these and other programs also differ in many ways. Most, for example, are set up with one-on-one relationships between a mentor and a mentee. In some programs, however, several individuals— including a mentor, sometimes several mentees, and other school representatives—collaborate to provide resources and support for beginning teachers. In some, as in Kentucky, mentors are paid for a fixed amount of time. In others, a stipend or other type of benefit is provided, and the mentor and mentee determine their own schedule. In a few programs, such as in Minneapolis, the mentorship is a full-time job conducted during a temporary leave from standard teaching responsibilities.

Despite their differences, successful mentoring programs have certain elements in common. Box 2.1 lists seven elements of a strong program.

BOX 2.1

Elements of a Strong Mentoring Program

1. Mentors are selected based on specific qualifications, including but not limited to their teaching ability. Listening skills and the ability to empathize with new teachers are only two of the many other necessary qualifications.

2. Mentors are provided with specific training for their role.

3. Mentors continue to receive support throughout the process, just as they give support to their mentees.

4. Mentors are paired with mentees based on criteria established within the program.

5. Mentors establish relationships with their mentees based on trust and respect.

6. Mentors receive some form of recognition for their work.

7. The mentoring program is evaluated and refined on an ongoing basis.

QUALIFICATIONS OF A GOOD MENTOR

Good teachers of children are not necessarily good teachers of adults. Although the obvious qualifications of skill in teaching and command of the curriculum are essential for a good mentor, they alone are not enough. Good mentors must also have a thorough understanding of both state and national standards. In addition, they must be sensitive to the needs of the beginning teacher, be able to transmit effective teaching strategies, be a good listener, be able to communicate openly with the beginning teacher, understand that teachers may be effective using a variety of styles, refrain from being judgmental, and model the philosophy that education is an ongoing process. Desirable personality traits include wisdom, caring, humor, and nurturing. Commitment to the profession is also essential.

In a survey of teacher-mentors within the San Francisco Unified School District (Jonson, 1999b), only 6 of 28 respondents mentioned professional teaching skills when asked what they considered to be the most important qualities in a good mentor. Nearly half mentioned "listening," with other frequently listed attributes including "supportive," "nonjudgmental," "positive," and "having a good sense of humor." One respondent summarized particularly well what most seemed to say: "I think what [the mentees] valued most was emotional support—though of course practical ideas are good—[also] sensitivity [and] knowledge of subject matter and methodologies."

Understanding of Standards. During the past 10 years, educators have struggled with establishing standards and with the challenges associated with standardized assessments. With passage of the No Child Left Behind (NCLB) Act in 2002 and with its pending reauthorization in 2007, tests and standards have played an increasingly prominent role in shaping curriculum. Although many have expressed concerns about overemphasizing testing and about misused tests, beginning teachers need to approach these standards with a clear focus. They need to start from the pragmatic premise that standards are of benefit for students.

Matt Gandal and Jennifer Vranek (2001) of Project Achieve, a bipartisan group created by U.S. governors and business leaders, argue that teaching a common body of essential skills and knowledge does not narrow the curriculum or inhibit good teaching practice. The more we expect from students, the more they will achieve, Gandal and Vranek note. From their examination of state and national policies, they have formulated what is needed for standards to have a positive impact: "teachable, parsimonious standards"; rich and rigorous tests that align with the standards; assistance and professional supports for teachers; and "a fighting chance for students"—extra help, more time, resources, whatever it takes to boost achievement (pp. 6–13).

Mentors can help beginning teachers understand that high and rigorous academic standards are

- a way to establish what all students need to know and be able to do;
- a result of a public and political outcry for increased accountability in schools;
- not yet well implemented in most schools, although not for lack of trying;
- fraught with challenges and difficulties but still an opportunity to raise the achievement of all; and
- a bipartisan reform that offers a common ground on which all advocates of good education can unite (Scherer, 2001, p. 5).

Sensitivity to the Needs of the Beginning Teacher. Understanding the needs of the beginning teacher is at the core of being an effective mentor. The mentor must be empathetic with the beginner and keep in mind that the mentee is still developing, both personally and professionally. Most experienced teachers remember those first years and the stresses of being new to the profession (see Chapter 3). Only those who can understand and empathize with the problems and concerns of the beginner—and who can keep in mind the basic skills required of all teachers (see Chapter 4)—are truly able to support the protégé, offer constructive assistance, and reduce rather than add to the beginning teacher's feeling of being overwhelmed. One of the San Francisco mentors surveyed noted as one of the most important qualifications for good mentoring simply "remembering my first year—with no one to help me along" (Jonson, 1999b).

Ability to Transmit Effective Teaching Strategies. No matter how successful teachers are in reaching young children, they will not make a good mentor unless they can also convey those strategies to the adult learner (see Chapters 6 and 7). Techniques for teaching adults include providing direct assistance, doing demonstration teaching, observing the mentee and providing feedback, role modeling, reflecting with the mentee, and discussing strategies formally in conferences or informally at other times in ways that are meaningful to another adult (see Chapter 8). As one San Francisco respondent noted, a good mentor is able to give "a wealth of practical strategies from which [mentees] can build their own system" (Jonson, 1999b).

Ability to Listen. Of the 28 San Francisco mentors who responded to a question about what they considered to be the most important qualifications for serving as a mentor, nearly half mentioned "listening" at or near the top of their lists. In fact, listening was the most frequently noted individual characteristic. In several cases, the respondent further pointed out that a mentor must have *time* to listen. Others coupled listening with giving support and encouragement.

All too often, the beginning teacher simply needs to talk to someone about what has happened during the day. Although this may not seem to be a difficult need to fill, working alone in the classroom does not leave open any possibility of discussing ideas during the routine workday. Sometimes the act of sitting by while the beginning teacher talks can itself help a protégé reflect on a situation and figure out what went well, what did not, and how things could have been done differently. At other times, mentors might help further by asking questions that then guide the beginning teachers to their own solutions, or the mentors might provide support simply by confirming the mentees' thoughts or letting them know that their concerns are valid or typical.

To listen well, a mentor should do the following:

- Listen quietly while displaying interest through eye contact, body language, and occasional brief comments such as "I see," "Really?" "Interesting," and so on.
- Invite further discussion or clarification when needed.
- Paraphrase important ideas to verify understanding.
- Listen actively; that is, note not only what the mentees are saying but also if they seem worried, confused, pleased, or enthusiastic.

Ability to Communicate Openly With the Beginning Teacher. Several San Francisco mentors cited communication skills as essential for good mentoring. Often they connected the idea of openness—a willingness to share experiences and materials with the mentee without reserve—with communication. Respondents sometimes followed or preceded the word *open* with *nonjudgmental* or *accessible,* other frequently noted mentor qualities.

According to J. B. Rowley (1999), a professor of education who has spent the past decade helping establish mentor programs, a primary requirement for good mentoring is the ability to communicate hope and optimism. He writes,

> Good mentor-teachers capitalize on opportunities to affirm the human potential of their mentees. They do so in private conversations and in public settings. Good mentors share their own struggles and frustrations and how they overcame them. And always, they do so in a genuine and caring way that engenders trust (Rowley, 1999, p. 22).

Understanding of Diverse Teaching Styles. It is important that a mentor have "the ability to recognize and nurture a beginning teacher in finding his own style, strengths, and weaknesses," according to one San Francisco mentor. Another mentor noted the importance of allowing the beginning teacher "space to discover her own teaching style while being close by in case the mentor is needed" (Jonson, 1999b). This same mentor felt it was important not to interfere with the instructional strategies established by the beginning teacher.

Each of these experienced mentors recognized the importance of providing support and assistance without attempting to impose an individual style on the beginning teacher. Only with such an understanding will beginning teachers have the opportunity to grow in their own personal ways. Glenn refers to the need for mentors to accept differences. In one mentor-mentee pairing, "both . . . teachers stated that they would not have changed their placement given the opportunity to do so; they came to accept that differences are inevitable and perhaps even useful" (2006, p. 93).

Restraint From Judgment. Experienced mentors agree that being nonjudgmental is key to the success of a mentor program. Only if beginning teachers believe they are not being judged will they be willing to share ideas, take risks, and develop their skills to the fullest. Mentees who feel that they are being judged or criticized are more likely to work with and talk about teaching techniques and processes that are comfortable, those that they feel they have already mastered to some extent. They are likely to feel vulnerable when discussing problems or concerns—which defeats the point of having a mentor in the first place.

If the mentor is nonjudgmental, on the other hand, the beginning teacher is more likely to admit difficulties and seek out the help so valuable in the mentor-mentee relationship. The beginning teacher is also more likely to experiment with new, more creative teaching techniques when in the presence of the mentor.

Along with being nonjudgmental, most—but not all—experienced mentors believe that mentors should not be involved in evaluation of the mentee in any way. Again, beginning teachers feel less vulnerable discussing problems and concerns with someone who will not later evaluate them. In many programs, in fact, confidentiality is considered essential and helps bring about trust between the mentor and the mentee.

Portner lists the following important differences between mentors and evaluators (1998, p. 6):

- Mentoring is collegial; evaluating is hierarchical.
- Mentoring is ongoing; evaluating visits are set by policy.
- Mentoring develops self-reliance; evaluating judges performance.
- Mentoring keeps data confidential; evaluating files it and makes it available.
- Mentoring uses data to reflect; evaluating uses it to judge.
- In mentoring, value judgments are made by the teacher; in evaluation, they are made by the supervisor.

In a few programs, like the one in Minneapolis, the mentor does play some role in evaluating the beginning teacher. The idea there is that the mentor knows the beginning teacher better than most other potential evaluators and that an assessment from a mentor is fairer than one from another evaluator might be. However, in the Minneapolis program, evaluation that might affect retention occurs only after the beginning teacher's third year in the profession.

The California Formative Assessment and Support System for Teachers (CFASST), a massive state-supported reform effort begun in 1999 to improve teaching, also involves assessment—but not for the purposes of retention decisions. At the core of the CFASST program are mentoring relationships, new teaching standards, and *formative* assessment tools—that is, assessment intended to help teachers improve practice, not to be used as a basis for formal teacher evaluation. CFASST, which grew out of the Santa Cruz New Teacher Project (discussed in detail in Chapter 5), requires that these assessments be implemented within the context of local programs to support beginning teachers. This structured, two-year professional developmental program was used in 133 BTSA programs across the state in 2002–2003. In this "nonjudgmental" mode, mentors and novice teachers reflect together on teaching in relation to student learning. Rather than evaluate the beginning teacher's effectiveness through cursory administrative observations and judgments, trained CFASST mentors team together with beginners to help them learn about best practices, plan lessons, reflect on teaching, and develop ways to apply what they have learned to their teaching.

Without a strong relationship built on common experience, trust, and a nonjudgmental stance, a mentoring program is not likely to succeed. In one California system, for example, coaches are hired to work with 15 to 18 new teachers at various schools throughout the district. "I was assigned a PAR [Peer Assistance Review] coach, who was not a peer because she doesn't teach elementary school, not an assistant because she never once offered to help in any way, and not a coach because she never modeled a single lesson plan for me or any of her first-year teachers at [my school]," said one discouraged beginning teacher (quoted in Harrington, 2001, p. 1). She and other beginning teachers in the PAR program have said that the coach seemed more like a judge than a mentor. After less than eight hours of observing the beginning teacher, the coach wrote an evaluation. The beginning teacher felt that the coach spent the year judging and criticizing her, despite the fact that the coach worked at a middle school (unlike the elementary school where the beginning teacher worked) and with a very different student population than the largely Hispanic and socioeconomically disadvantaged population at her elementary school (Harrington, 2001, p. 1).

Modeling of Continuous Learning. One of the key ideas behind any mentor-mentee program is that learning is a continuous process, not a finite experience that ends with the receipt of a diploma on graduation from an accredited teacher education program. Mentoring is one way to provide beginning teachers with continuing education specific to their situations. It is crucial that mentors model for the new teacher the importance of continuing education by partaking in further learning themselves.

Being a mentor is in itself a means of continuing to learn. The mentor-teacher can get new ideas from the novice teacher—just as Nancy learned a new attention-getting technique from Dolores—and should not be afraid to let the beginning teacher know this. In addition, the mentor can (a) attend workshops, conferences, and graduate classes, sometimes with the mentee, sometimes with the aid of mentor program funding designated for such career development; (b) experiment with new methods, sometimes inspired by the mentee; and (c) write and read articles, sometimes in response to issues that arise within the mentor-mentee relationship.

Mentors should admit to the beginning teacher that they do not have the answers to every question and problem that arise. Mentors, like the mentee, can always learn from others and should be comfortable sharing questions with their mentees. The admission that their mentor, too, is still learning can be encouraging to beginning teachers, who may be relieved to find that they are not the only person without all the answers. This in itself can be reassuring to a struggling beginner.

EFFECTIVE TRAINING

In February 1997, the U.S. Department of Education's National Center for Education Statistics published its report, *Teacher Professionalization and Teacher Commitment: A Multilevel Analysis.* According to that report, having a mentor program to assist beginning teachers is less important than the quality of that assistance for improving teacher performance and commitment (Portner, 1998, p. 4). In other words, a mentor program is much more helpful if it's well thought out. A formal, high-quality program is significantly more likely to be effective than a program in which the mentor is simply assigned to a mentee and then set loose.

Mentoring requires commitment to the program, and this is sometimes best attained when the mentor has a clear definition of the roles and responsibilities required. In effective programs, mentors receive at the outset a specific description of these roles and responsibilities. They may receive relevant reading materials to get them started as well. They also receive some level of formal training.

Training might be conducted by a program coordinator (a sort of "mentors' mentor") or by a school administrator. This leader sets up conferences and workshops to discuss techniques, goals, skills, and attitudes. Although some of this training should happen before work actually begins with the beginning teachers, training should continue after mentors have formed a working relationship with their mentees.

MENTOR SUPPORT

Supporting new teachers is complex and demanding work, and rarely intuitive. Exemplary classroom educators do not always become outstanding teacher educators. Veteran teachers stepping forward to mentor beginning colleagues need time, careful training, and ongoing support to develop new skills and understandings that will enable them to become talented teachers of teachers (Santa Cruz New Teacher Center Web site, http://www.newteachercenter.org).

The Santa Cruz New Teacher Center, which posts the preceding information on its Web site, is considered to be one of the best such centers in the state, and some consider it to be one of the best in the nation. To follow through on its belief that mentors need support, the center provides access to many resources and much information on its Web site.

Five mentors in Marin County, California, also stress the importance of support in their work. To have a successful program, they say, support providers should meet regularly with each other to discuss successes and questions and to talk about teaching (Smith, 1993, p. 15). Three of the five mentors in Marin County did not feel they had been supported in their role and named this lack of support as their chief concern and source of anxiety about the program (Smith, 1993, p. 14).

Like the beginning teacher (and even the experienced teacher), the beginning mentor (and even the experienced mentor) needs to discuss issues with other mentors or with a program coordinator. Support must be ongoing and readily available. In some districts, mentors may meet in support groups to discuss problems and questions. A program coordinator or other administrator should also be available to discuss issues as needed and to help locate resources for the mentor, both generally and when specifically requested. In some districts, an experienced mentor may observe a beginning mentor in action, just as the beginning mentor (experienced teacher) observes a beginning teacher in action. Finally, some districts publish a mentor newsletter dealing with issues of concern to the readership (Smith, 1993, p. 15). The newsletter could also commend the work of mentors and beginning teachers as a reward for good work and a source of ideas for others.

In addition to emotional and educational support, more practical types of support are also necessary for a program to work effectively. Most important, *time* must be provided for this important duty. This could be in the form of a substitute teacher releasing the mentor from the classroom to be with the beginning teacher, or it could mean release time from non-teaching responsibilities, such as playground or hall duty. A program can also be strengthened significantly by funding for workshops and training, both in the field of mentoring itself and in areas relevant for the beginning teacher. (For more about finding time to mentor, see Chapter 9, Overcoming Obstacles and Reaping the Rewards.)

MENTOR-TO-MENTEE PAIRING

Matches between mentors and mentees are sometimes based on convenience and availability. In a small program, in fact, there may be little choice of mentors for a beginning teacher. Ideally, however, there should be established criteria for pairing the beginning teacher with a mentor who will serve as the richest learning resource available. These criteria might include the following:

- Proximity
- Same or close grade level
- Same or related subject area
- Common lunch or planning period
- Similar personality or educational philosophy

Experts disagree regarding this last criterion. Some believe that a mentor who understands and believes in the beginning teacher's philosophies and styles will be better able to help and that the relationship will be more comfortable if both partners share educational beliefs. Others say that two teachers will learn more from each other if they have different styles (ASCD, 1999a, p. 109).

According to the San Francisco mentors surveyed (Jonson 1999b), proximity is a particularly relevant issue for effectiveness of the pairing. Of 27 mentors who responded to a question about whether their mentees were likely to come to them or to someone else for assistance, 24 said their mentees came to them in at least some cases. The three who did not get questions from their mentees all cited location as the problem: Beginning teachers were more likely to go first to someone nearby, they said. One other respondent said that, of four mentees, two were on-site and came first to the mentor, but the other two, at different sites, talked to someone else first.

Even of those who said their mentees *were* likely to come to them, one qualified the response by explaining, "Mentees need instantaneous assistance sometimes and will first seek help at their own school site. If the problem doesn't need immediate solution—they then seek help from me." Another wrote, "For resources . . . and also for class management/discipline [the mentee comes to me]. It is more convenient for the mentee to confer with site staff for logistics." Yet another wrote, "It depends on the issue. It is very common for teachers to go to the *closest* teacher (i.e., next door) for simple questions. I think my mentees seek me out for more challenging issues" (Jonson, 1999b).

All in all, 10 respondents mentioned proximity as an issue in how frequently the mentee consulted the mentor for advice. One even mentioned that having different lunch periods was a problem. Four said that teaching at different grade levels prevented them from working together on all issues. Teachers working in different-level schools are even less likely to have a successful relationship. Kindergarten, first-grade, and even fifth-grade teachers, for example, face very different challenges than do single-subject teachers of teenagers at high schools.

Mentor-mentee matches are often made by a principal and other committee members who have interviewed the teachers involved. A program coordinator who has worked with the mentor also often has insights regarding appropriate pairings. Pairings are made very early in a beginning teacher's career, however, often before that teacher's needs and strengths are realized. Occasionally, even with strong mentors, the match does not serve the needs of the beginning teacher as expected. If this happens, a good system should have built into it some way for a new pairing to be made without any blame placed (ASCD, 1999a, p. 110). Program coordinators should never lose sight of the focus: to provide beginning teachers with the most help possible to enable them to make a transition to the professional world during their first years on the job.

ESTABLISHMENT OF THE MENTOR-MENTEE RELATIONSHIP

For a mentor-mentee relationship to be most effective, the beginning teacher and the mentor must get along both personally and professionally. According to research, the success of a relationship is generally based on two factors: (a) whether the protégé respects the mentor as a person and (b) whether the protégé admires the mentor's knowledge, experience, and style (Jonson, 1997, p. 9).

If the beginning teacher is assigned to a mentor who is critical, excessively task oriented, uncaring, and unpredictable, that new teacher will be concerned primarily with gaining the favor of the mentor and avoiding criticism. If, on the other hand, the mentor has developed a trusting relationship with the beginning teacher—one in which the mentor has proven to be safe, predictable, and supportive—the protégé is more likely to take risks, to try new ideas, and to develop new skills with the mentor's aid (ASCD, 1999a, p. 95). In the example at the beginning of this chapter,

Dolores and Nancy seem to have a compatible and collegial relationship. It is this type of trusting, positive, productive relationship that every mentor needs to strive for from the very beginning of a relationship.

In fact, *trust* was the most common word used by San Francisco mentors to explain why they thought their mentees came to them for assistance. Other elements considered important for a successful mentor-mentee relationship were having an outgoing personality, being cheerful and helpful, being willing to let mentees try their own solutions, and letting the mentee know that any communications would be kept confidential. Box 2.2 offers some tips for establishing a good relationship with a mentee.

BOX 2.2

Tips for Establishing a Strong Mentor-Mentee Relationship

The following advice is based on responses from San Francisco mentors to a question asking how they built trusting relationships with their mentees:

- Have regular contact, both formal and informal. Let mentees know that you are there for them.
- Build trust based on respect, open communication, and support. Attempt to offer as much of these qualities as possible.
- Make regular phone calls. Share unit plans and resources.
- Let mentees know that they can be open and honest with their needs.
- Have informal visits and conversations. Socialize. Be available in a timely manner.
- Try to be nonjudgmental and open. Never talk about new teachers behind their backs.
- Listen. Respond to their questions. Provide a variety of resources.
- Validate the challenges of teaching. Take mentees' ideas and feelings seriously. Help them trust their own judgment.
- Discuss problems realistically and let them know that you have the same problems sometimes. Let them vent.
- Hold meetings for new teachers at the school. Focus in part on school activities, but mostly allow the meetings to be open-ended so the teachers can bring concerns and questions as well as stories of success.
- Offer support. Be positive. Ask what they need.
- Talk with mentees. Share materials and resources. Get together with them socially. Take an active interest in their classrooms.
- Tell the mentee at the first meeting that whatever is said goes no further. Be warm and caring. Share your own experiences as a teacher—good and bad.
- Be accessible. Be willing to diverge from your agenda and help in areas the mentee feels are more pressing.
- Treat mentees as your peers. Confide in them. Talk frankly, openly, and honestly.
- Show that it is a mutually beneficial relationship—the mentee benefits from your experience, and you benefit from their exuberance and technology skills.
- Observe together. Talk about areas other than teaching. Joke. Let the mentee know your strengths and weaknesses.
- Be available, open, and honest. Be reliable and follow through with activities.

Although experts seem to agree universally that the nature of the relationship is key to the success of the mentoring program, creating the required trust in the beginning, when time to socialize is limited, can be difficult. How does one get to know a beginning teacher at the start of a year, when so many tasks are required—from setting up the room to getting to know the children to finalizing or adjusting curriculum?

Some suggestions for building a relationship with a beginning teacher early in the year include eating lunch together, taking a trip to a teacher supply store, sharing family pictures, bringing the beginning teacher a cup of coffee in the morning or a soda after school and sitting to have a chat, touring the school together, or taking a drive around the school neighborhood. That first day when the children arrive can itself be overwhelming to a new teacher, and having someone experienced to turn to can help get things off to a good start (see Appendix A, First-Day Checklist). The ASCD (1999a, p. 92) also suggests the following tips for mentors wanting to get a relationship off to a good start:

1. Prepare your classroom early so you have time available when the beginning teacher needs your help.

2. While working with beginning teachers to set up their rooms, use the time to talk and identify their biggest short-term concerns. Set up times to work together to accomplish these tasks. This effort will demonstrate to beginning teachers that you will be there at "crunch time."

3. While cutting out letters for bulletin boards or arranging desks, talk about each other's family, background, and teaching dreams. This will reduce the beginning teacher's stress, help begin to build a relationship, and allow you to address some critical needs.

In addition to getting to know the beginning teacher in general, the mentor should try to learn something about the mentee's expectations of the program. Some beginning teachers—like some students—are hungry to learn, eager for advice. Others are defensive at first (Rowley, 1999, p. 21), resistant to assistance. Regardless of personality, the mentor must work with the beginning teacher, adapting to the style and needs of the individual. See Chapter 9, Overcoming Obstacles and Reaping the Rewards, for tips on working with difficult mentees.

The frequency of mentor-mentee meetings varies, depending on how the program is set up. Portner recommends getting together every day or two for the first two weeks, then about once every week or two for the rest of the first semester, and less often during the rest of the year (2001, p. 57). In programs where the mentor has full release from other teaching responsibilities, weekly meetings are possible and expected. For others, finding the necessary time can be difficult but is essential. See Chapter 9, Overcoming Obstacles and Reaping the Rewards, for tips on managing time to work with mentees.

RECOGNITION OF SERVICE

For any program to be successful, the participants need to feel recognized and valued. Chapter 9, Overcoming Obstacles and Reaping the Rewards, discusses in more detail the many benefits of serving as a mentor. It is important to note here, however, that although some of the biggest benefits are in personal and professional growth and self-satisfaction for the mentor, a good program should also have built into it tangible rewards (see Box 2.3).

BOX 2.3

Possible Rewards to Recognize Mentor Service

- Reduced class size
- Opportunity to team-teach with a protégé
- Release from other duties (e.g., hall or yard duty)
- Paid attendance at conferences or workshops
- Graduate-school tuition
- An end-of-year recognition banquet or luncheon
- A formal recognition ceremony before the board of education or school faculty
- A stipend

Whatever the specific program, no system should take for granted the time and contribution of a good mentor. The mentor's enthusiasm and contribution to the school must be recognized if the program is to be successful, just as beginning teachers must feel appreciated if they are to continue in their role. Continuity will keep the program strong and ensure the growth that comes with experience.

PROGRAM EVALUATION

Mentoring programs are only one of many strategies used for professional development. Just as with other strategies, evaluation needs to be built into these programs from their inception, and evidence must be gathered throughout the process to determine their effectiveness (Guskey, 2000). In the first year of a new program, evaluators should assess the operation of the program: Is implementation occurring as expected? How could it be improved? Over the next few years, the focus should move to achievement of goals and purposes: Is the retention rate for beginning teachers improving? Are both beginning and experienced teachers gaining new knowledge, skills, and strategies? Are collegiality and collaboration among faculty increasing? Are students learning more (Portner, 2001, p. 84)?

Structured interviews, observations, and surveys are all good techniques for gathering information to be used for program evaluation. Other sources of information might include teachers' journal entries, informal or formal discussions, and questionnaires administered to both mentors and mentees (Portner, 2001, p. 92). The information gathered can then be used as a basis for improving the program through constant fine-tuning and modification. In addition, this information is important for accountability purposes and should affect decisions regarding continuation of the program (p. 89).

ALTERNATIVE MENTOR PROGRAMS

Although the one-to-one pairing discussed throughout this chapter is typical of new teacher-mentor programs, a single teacher may not have the time to help the beginner as needed. Variations on this setup are sometimes necessary and can also be effective. For example, new teachers may work with one mentor on curriculum and with another to help them become comfortable with district procedures. In another variation, a non-local mentor may be available to a new teacher on an ongoing basis through e-mail correspondence.

The following setups enable new teachers to benefit from mentoring in a variety of forms.

Multiple Mentoring

In some districts, one mentee may have two or more mentors. Mentors can divide responsibilities by the type of guidance or simply by time. With this setup, neither mentor needs to devote as much time as a single pairing requires. The setup also allows two mentors, both familiar with the new teacher, to problem-solve regarding issues. As with a single mentor, issues might need to be kept confidential within the triad—but this arrangement allows a new teacher to benefit from the help of more than one veteran.

Support Groups

Although a one-to-one mentor-mentee relationship is key to a good mentoring program, new teachers may also meet together in discussion groups with a seasoned facilitator. Often these groups meet about once a month, and teachers discuss such specific topics as what to do during the first three weeks of school, how to incorporate a particular set of state standards, or how to conduct a parent-teacher conference (Portner, 2001, pp. 93–94).

E-Mentoring

As in many other areas, technology can play a large role in helping teachers help other teachers. Techniques and tools are sometimes used to supplement other mentoring efforts—but in other cases, distance mentors work with new teachers using primarily technological tools. The New Teacher Center Formative Assessment System (NTC FAS), a part of the Santa Cruz New Teacher Project discussed in Chapter 5, is one example of technology use in mentoring. In this computerized system, mentors use a framework and tools to help beginning teachers. Teachers may access files at their convenience and use tools such as search and sort to work with the files (Duncan, 2005, p. 8). Other examples of technology used in mentoring follow:

Online Professional Development. Online modules provide new teachers with video clips and other resources to help them learn about such topics as classroom management and working with English Language Learners. Clips include demonstrations of effective practice, discussions among beginning and veteran teachers, and so on. Teachers can view the programs at their convenience (Duncan, 2005, p. 8).

Communication and Interaction. Teachers communicate through e-mail and also using "chat," which allows real-time communication with a record being made of any discussion (Duncan, 2005, pp. 8–9).

Collaborative Workspace. Mentors and beginning teachers post, store, and share work in workspace environments and even work in real-time on digital whiteboards. They can interact, communicate, videoconference, and create professional portfolios in shared space (Duncan, 2005, p. 9).

Information and Data Management. Teachers store data online for analysis and utilization (Duncan, 2005, p. 9). A wealth of Internet sites provide information for teachers on a wide variety of instructional topics.

E-BEST. Connecticut has used "E-BEST communications" as part of its Beginning Educator Support and Training (BEST) program to create a statewide e-mail network of beginning teachers by content area. Project leaders and teachers-in-residence use this Listserv to regularly communicate with beginning teachers about teaching resources, professional development, and critical issues around the BEST portfolio.

FIRSTTech. The state of Louisiana has established a network and support system among teachers called FIRSTTech. As a part of the state's mentoring program, Louisiana posts training materials and links to teacher resources on a blackboard Web site. New teachers also participate on the site in online discussions about teaching.

CONCLUSION

In the scenario at the beginning of this chapter, Nancy was able to help Dolores see her own strengths and to offer suggestions for furthering Dolores's development as a beginning teacher. The Virginia program in which these two teachers participated was well structured, and the pairing between the teachers was good.

Although individual programs throughout the country vary, all successful ones include some common elements. This chapter looked at seven successful programs and discussed key elements for effective mentoring. One of those elements was that mentors are selected based on specific qualifications, including the ability to empathize with beginning teachers. Chapter 3 serves to remind the experienced teacher of the many stresses common for teaching professionals as they begin their new careers. It is certain to increase mentors' empathy as they work with beginning teachers. Chapter 4 looks in more detail at the skills new teachers need to move toward professionalism. Chapter 5 looks at the broader notion of induction programs as they are designed to help new teachers, and it also discusses mentoring programs designed specifically to help teachers progress professionally.

> The mentor relationship is one of the most developmentally important relationships a person can have in early adulthood.
>
> —Daniel Levinson, *Seasons of a Man's Life* (1986)

3

Remembering the First Days

As a newly hired teacher, I recall being shown to my classroom just prior to the beginning of school. There were four blank walls, some boxes of crayons, rulers, paper, and a few textbooks in the room. After unlocking the door, the smiling secretary waved good-bye and wished me good luck! A thick lump formed at the back of my throat and started spreading downward. I was totally alone and, although I was trained in a fine university program, the enormity of organizing the bits and pieces into a learning environment eluded me. The thought of being responsible for thirty small children for the next nine months nearly panicked me.

—Leila Christenbury (1995, p. 3)

To understand the role of the mentor in education, it is helpful for mentors to think back to some of their own first-year teaching experiences and the anxieties they felt. The fears of the teacher quoted here are common to many novices to the profession, and most veterans will probably remember similar experiences if they try. Before meeting with the beginning teacher, a mentor should try to recall these things: What was that first year like? What caused anxiety? What unexpected problems arose? How were they resolved? Did any particular individual help out? If so, was that individual assigned to help you, or did a sympathetic colleague simply take the initiative to become involved? How did it feel to be new to the job? How would it have been if no one had stepped in? Or, if no one did step in, how could things have been different if someone had?

Entering the teaching profession presents challenges not experienced in any other field. Only a teacher carries the same load in the first year as an experienced colleague carries—and sometimes under even more difficult circumstances. Only a teacher works completely isolated from other professionals, responsible for a roomful of children, with students and parents alike expecting the same proficiency as from the 20-year veteran.

Researchers Brown and Williams (1977), Ryan (1986), and Bush (1996), have outlined the following characteristics typical of the first year in the teaching profession:

- A beginning teacher's job description is essentially the same as the teacher's down the hall who has 5, 10, or even 15 years of experience.
- Teaching is generally done in isolation. The system does not encourage observation of others' teaching, the sharing of ideas, or group lesson planning.
- Beginning teachers often get the most-difficult-to-teach students and other "hand-me-downs" of the system: old textbooks, desks, and schedules.
- Teaching must be experienced to be clearly understood. Sitting at a student's desk for 16 years does not give a true picture of what teaching is really like.
- Student teaching experiences, in general, are not extensive enough to provide a teacher with the full breadth of experiences necessary to be a master teacher.

All too often, beginning teachers find themselves doing the jobs that others have discarded. They end up teaching the class sections nobody else wants; are rotated into certain duties that others know enough to avoid; and are given the least attractive, most awkwardly appointed classrooms (Moran, 1990, p. 213). Middle and high school teachers may end up teaching classes in a variety of subject areas, regardless of their area of focus. One new middle school teacher, for instance, found herself planning for two math, one social science, and two physical education classes.

Given these circumstances, no matter how thorough the beginning teacher's preparation has been—no matter how "ready" that teacher feels on the first day of school—it probably isn't enough. Figure 3.1 shows just some of the problems beginning teachers are likely to face. Yet despite the confusion so soon encountered, beginning teachers are often reluctant to ask colleagues for help because they fear that they might be considered incompetent. They might refrain from asking principals for advice because they worry that exposing their difficulties could lead to a negative evaluation. "It is professional suicide to admit you need help," one beginning teacher said (Pearson & Honig, 1992, p. 5). "You learn this fast so you don't go up to your department chair or other teachers for help."

Figure 3.1   Problems confronting new teachers

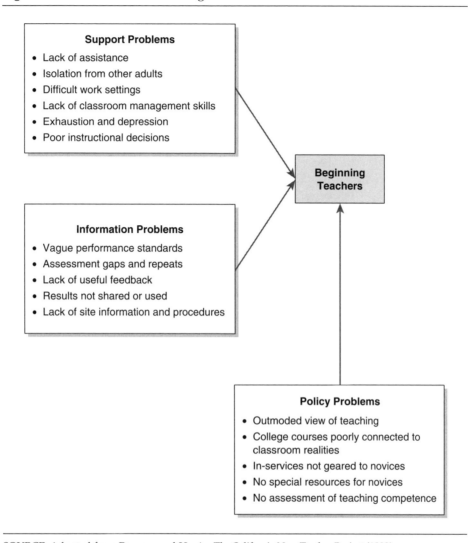

SOURCE: Adapted from Pearson and Honig, *The California New Teacher Project* (1992).

Even if a beginning teacher does want to consult professionally with an experienced colleague, a busy day may make that impossible; struggling onward might seem to be a better use of time. All too often, without an effective induction program, the beginning teacher muddles through, sometimes surviving, sometimes leaving the profession in frustration. Without communicating with other teachers, the beginning teacher may not realize that these frustrations are typical, that others have the same problems with discipline and management.

PRESERVICE TRAINING

"The oldest myth about teacher preparation still prevails—that newly certified teachers are fully prepared for the rigor and complexity of classroom instruction," writes Sheila W. Moran (1990, p. 211), former director of the Upper Valley Teacher Training Program in Lebanon, New Hampshire. She continues,

> Preservice education, even at its most intense and pragmatic, can only begin the process of scientific discovery and artistic creativity that is teaching. Newly certified teachers, however bright and capable, are just ready to begin the meaningful learning that occurs during the first few years of true professional engagement (Moran, 1990, p. 211).

Bartell (1995, p. 28) points out that university coursework builds a teacher's conceptual understanding, and clinical or field experience helps prepare the teacher for the reality of the classroom. But classroom knowledge itself comes only from experience in the classroom environment (Doyle, 1990). "No matter what initial professional preparation they receive," writes Bartell (1995, p. 29), "teachers are never fully prepared for classroom realities and for the responsibilities associated with meeting the needs of a rapidly growing, increasingly diverse student population."

A significant majority of the new teachers surveyed for a Public Agenda report noted that their preservice training had included "too little about the nuts and bolts of teaching: how to run classrooms, maintain discipline, deal with the routine pressures of their profession and even how to teach effectively" (Raspberry, 2000, p. 3). None of the teachers surveyed had been in the business of teaching for more than five years. In contrast, of 900 education professors interviewed in the same study, 37% did not believe that it was important to teach teachers how to maintain discipline and order in the classroom. The problem is not a lack of concern from the professors, according to Public Agenda President Deborah Wadsworth, but rather,

> They have a very different mind-set. They . . . seem to assume a sort of glorified environment in which every youngster comes to school problem-free and eager. . . . They are almost tone-deaf to the things the young classroom teachers are telling us they need (Raspberry, 2000, p. 3).

The California Commission on the Teaching Profession reports that the coursework required for a teaching credential is poorly connected both to current theory about how to teach and to the reality of teaching in a classroom. In addition, "the teacher's workplace is organized and supervised in ways that isolate and hobble teachers," it states. "Qualities that are seen as hallmarks of productivity in business—mutual help, exchange of ideas, cooperative work to develop better practices—are rare in schools" (Pearson & Honig, 1992, p. 11).

In a San Diego County study, all of 15 new middle and high school teachers interviewed noted that the actual practice of teaching was often inconsistent with the theory they had learned in their coursework. "Student teaching and actual teaching are such completely different experiences," one explained. "When I was student teaching, someone was always there for me if I needed them. Now, I'm expected to know everything and do everything right and I know I'm not doing it right. I feel like the rope got cut and I'm floating. Actually, sometimes I feel like I'm falling" (Mathison, 1996, p. 16).

Repeatedly, recent research has indicated that quality education for teachers *does* lead to quality teachers, which in turn leads to better performance for students (Darling-Hammond, 2001, 2003; Hoffman, 2004; International Reading Association, 2003; Laczko-Kerr & Berliner, 2002; Wilson, Floden, & Ferrini-Mundy, 2001). The problem is not that preservice teacher training is ineffective, but rather that it is not sufficient; support needs to continue after the teacher begins practice in the work setting. As Hoffman writes, "Investing in teacher education needs to consist of more than just improving initial preparation. Investment must reach deeply into lifelong professional development" (2004, p. 127).

Rarely do teachers anticipate the extreme gulf they will find between their training and reality. Most begin their first assignments feeling prepared and having high expectations for themselves and their students. Given the stress of their first year, however, they often lose confidence in themselves and their abilities when they find that their preparation has not been adequate. It is then that they need someone to turn to and someone to offer support.

THE NEED FOR WARM BODIES

The problems of beginning teachers are exacerbated for those who lack preservice preparation altogether. A growing number of beginning teachers are coming to the classroom without the training that leads to a teaching credential. Because of the shortage of qualified teachers, 30 states now permit hiring teachers on temporary or emergency licenses (Hoffman, 2004, p. 120). In Los Angeles, for example, more than half of the new teachers hired for the 2000–2001 school year lacked a certificate. About one-fourth of *all* district teachers went to work with only emergency credentials (Gursky, 2000). In places like Los Angeles, the shortage of teachers has reached epic proportions. "The problem is getting worse, not better," says Doug Scott, spokesperson for the California Department of Education. "This is not a shortage. This is a crisis. We are literally attacking it as if we were in round-the-clock combat" (Gursky, 2000, p. 11).

Furthermore, the shortage of qualified teachers has a particularly strong impact on students in impoverished districts. Los Angeles teachers lacking certification, for example, were concentrated in schools with the most disadvantaged students (Gursky, 2000, p. 11). According to *Quality Counts 2003*, a report commissioned and published by *Education Week* (Hoffman, 2004, p. 121),

- In California, 23% of teachers in the lowest achieving schools in 2000–2001 lacked full credentials, compared with 6% of teachers in the highest achieving schools.
- In Missouri, a disproportionate share of new teachers and of teachers with low ACT scores find employment in high-poverty, high-minority districts.
- In New York, fewer than half of the teachers in some high-poverty, high-minority schools from 1984 through 2000 were fully certified in all courses they taught.

All of these statistics point to a situation in which the children most in need of well-qualified teachers are the least likely to get them. At the same time, demographic characteristics of schools are changing, creating new challenges for teachers. In California, for example, students filling the classrooms come with nearly 140 different languages and with many national and cultural backgrounds (Moir, *Putting New Teachers at the Center*, p. 1). The teachers positioned in these schools, some of whom do not have a credential, face ever-increasing demands to help these children meet educational standards.

The future is likely only to bring more such problems. As school enrollments grow and as more teachers retire, the nation faces a huge challenge in training, hiring, and retaining enough teachers. Furthermore, the move to reduce class sizes in many states and districts has increased the demand for teachers. California, with its high-profile statewide class-reduction initiative, is a textbook example. Class-size reduction has caused districts to hire huge numbers of uncertified teachers, which threatens to dilute the positive impact of smaller classes. California needs to hire 300,000 new teachers during the next decade, and an estimated two million new teachers will be needed to staff our schools nationwide within the first 10 years of the 21st century (Bush, 2001).

Commentators such as Arthur Levine, president of Teacher's College, warn that the increasing need for teachers is colliding with simultaneous efforts to toughen hiring requirements (Levine, 1999). With the federal No Child Left Behind Act of 2001, all states are required to ensure that teachers of core academic subjects are highly qualified to teach those subjects. Yet many of these classrooms are staffed by teachers working with emergency or provisional certificates. In a nationwide study by Public Agenda, most school administrators reported facing at least some type of teacher shortage, and two-thirds (66%) said they have had to expend extra effort in recent years to recruit the teachers they need. Nationwide, urban educators report feeling the crunch more than educators in suburban districts. More than twice as many urban educators (26% urban, compared with 11% suburban) said they are facing a critical, widespread shortage, and a large majority (78%) said they have had to undertake extra recruiting efforts (Farkas et al., 2000).

How, then, can teachers be helped to build the professional skills necessary for teaching? And how can they get the support that will make them want to remain in high-poverty schools, as well as others? This need for "warm bodies" often provides the context for mentoring beginning teachers as classroom staff. Many of those teachers with emergency or provisional certificates especially require assistance as they jump unprepared into the profession. Even more than fully trained teachers, these emergency teachers are in danger of becoming overwhelmed and discouraged without the help of an experienced colleague.

REALITY SHOCK

Literature on beginning teachers outlines the stages of teacher development (Moir, 1999), beginning with the induction stage, or the first few years of teaching. This stage has been identified as a unique and important time in a teacher's career. During the induction period, first-year teachers generally experience what Ryan (1986) labeled *reality shock:* the transition from being a student who learns about teaching to actually being a teacher. Reality shock may be experienced in a variety of ways and to different degrees, depending on the individual. Preparation, familiarity with the setting of the first job, and difficulty of the teaching assignment may all affect the degree of shock.

Studies of beginning-teacher development continue to document that the early years of teaching are difficult and stressful and fail to enable the careful, thoughtful development of teaching expertise (Bullough, 1990; Darling-Hammond, 1988; Huling-Austin, 1987, 1992). Most beginning teachers experience daily classroom responsibility as a baptism by fire; many, over the course of their first year, lose faith in their own efficacy and in the learning potential of their students. Beginning teachers typically report worrying about "their kids" every waking hour and may even dream about them. "I feel overwhelmed," one beginning teacher wrote in a journal. "I knew teaching was a tough job, but nothing could have prepared me for all these problems and pitfalls."

It is easy to document that teachers' work environments are less than optimal, contributing to beginning-teacher "reality shock." Mentors—as well as superintendents and site administrators—need to think carefully about five workplace factors inherent in the professional lives of beginning teachers: the legacy of the one-room schoolhouse, inverse beginner responsibilities, restricted choices, invisibility and isolation, and a lack of professional dialogue.

The Legacy of the One-Room Schoolhouse. The vestige of pioneer times— when most schools had one teacher, one group of students, within one confined area—is still evident in most schools today. In many cases, the one-room schoolhouse is repeated every few yards down the school corridor. In these schools, so-called egg-carton schools, each teacher works within a separate, insulated hole. Many teachers believe, "This is *my* classroom, *my* professional world; these are *my* students, *my* materials—and others should leave me alone."

Unfortunately, the isolation stemming from this legacy inhibits professional growth for many teachers. "It masks the starkly different results achieved by different teachers," writes Schmoker (2006, p. 24).

> Without any point of comparison, the isolated teacher never has to confront the fact that (1) the teacher next door may be three times as effective as [she is], or (2) much of [her] teaching is inferior. . . . The upshot: isolation ensures that highly unprofessional practices are tolerated and thus proliferate in the name of . . . professionalism.

In contrast, recent school reform movements have demonstrated that teachers in successful schools are more likely to speak of "*our* students, *our* materials, *our* goals, and what *we* are trying to do." Beginning teachers are more likely to prosper in open, collaborative environments.

Inverse Beginner Responsibilities. Too often, experienced teachers protect their own turf and pass the leftovers on to new teachers. Often when a teacher resigns or retires, the teachers remaining in the school descend on the classroom to remove materials, equipment, and furniture of value and replace it with their own discards. The new teacher thus enters a classroom equipped with what no one else wanted. This situation extends even to students themselves; some administrators, faced with a vocal and demanding tenured staff, end up assigning the most difficult and lowest achieving students to the beginning teacher. All in all, beginning teachers are often left with the most demanding students and with picked-over classrooms. The message to beginning teachers is, "Welcome to teaching. Let's see if you can make it."

Restricted Choices. In many states and school districts, the working lives of teachers are too often bureaucratic and restricted. Teachers have few choices. Their schedules are set, and beginning teachers especially are told what, when, and how to teach. Their input is not solicited. With the current nationwide movement toward standards and testing—minimum competencies, mandated curriculum, and externally developed policies—teachers' professional lives are filled with even more mandates and less choice. Goodlad (1984) reported in his classic nationwide study *A Place Called School* that teachers had virtually no involvement in school-wide decisions.

Invisibility and Isolation. Glickman (1985) reported that only 50% of all experienced teachers have ever been observed for purposes of instructional improvement, and only 24% have been observed by another teacher in their school. This pattern changed somewhat in the 1980s and 1990s, when principals were encouraged to be "instructional leaders." This paradigm is now being challenged, however, as teachers question how appropriate it is for principals to serve dual roles, supervising teachers in a management capacity (e.g., evaluating their performance) and also trying to help them improve instruction.

Lack of Professional Dialogue. Because most classrooms are closed off from one another, teachers rarely talk together as professionals. Researchers have reported that professional talk among teachers lasts less than two minutes per day (Glickman, 1985). Teachers spend an overwhelming amount of their time talking to students and socializing with each other, but little time solving instructional problems together.

In attempting to struggle through these inherent blocks to teacher development in their work environments, conscientious beginning teachers may become consumed by the daily responsibilities of teaching. "When I first started teaching high-school English, I was not very good at it," one beginning teacher recalls,

> And I knew it. I hoped, though, that no one else would find out before I had a chance to fix things, and so I kept my door to my classroom firmly shut. I didn't want other teachers in my room; I didn't want administrators or parents. Because I knew I was stumbling and lurching through my lesson plans, I didn't even want to talk about what I was doing—or thinking of doing—in my classroom. (Christenbury, 1995, p. 3)

FEARS AND ANXIETIES OF BEGINNING TEACHERS

Many veteran teachers have vivid memories of their first-year teaching experiences, some of them intensely emotional. The often-voiced contention that the first year is one of trauma, drama, and basic survival may be overstated, but all beginning teachers do have special needs, problems, and concerns.

"The first months and years of teaching are full of pain, confusion, loneliness, and often humiliation," writes Moran (1990, p. 211). In thinking back, most teachers recall particular frustrations with classroom management and discipline and with time management issues. Researchers have identified other crucial issues as well (see Box 3.1). All these issues create stress for the beginning teacher. If left unchecked, this stress can lead to fatigue, and eventually the teacher may choose to leave the profession. But with the help of a good mentor, the beginning teacher can take hold of these issues, rise to the challenge, and move forward.

BOX 3.1

Areas of Particular Concern for Beginning Teachers

- Classroom management and discipline
- Time management
- An overwhelming workload
- Classroom instruction
- Technology in the classroom
- High-stakes accountability
- Sociocultural awareness and sensitivity
- Student motivation
- A solitary work environment
- Relationships with parents and colleagues

Classroom Management and Discipline

One of the biggest sources of teacher anxiety, classroom management is the ongoing task of keeping control in the room. Because teachers cannot anticipate the many behavioral events that will occur in their classroom, the beginning teacher often feels unprepared and out of control when they take place. Beginning teachers may feel incompetent when they don't know how to handle discipline and may experience particular anxiety when they cannot control disruptions. In many studies, teachers have noted specifically that they felt classroom management and discipline procedures should be given much more attention in the preservice curriculum (e.g., Mathison, 1996, p. 15).

Teachers have good reason for this concern. In 11 of 15 classrooms observed in the San Diego study of new teachers, researchers found that the general classroom environment was "uncontrolled and chaotic. Students were observed passing notes, holding private conversations, sleeping, and/or generally 'goofing off.'" In a survey of 63 teachers in that same study, 48% said they were often frustrated by the level of talking and general commotion in the classroom, and 24% sometimes felt that they spent most of the class period getting students to settle down (Mathison, 1996, pp. 13–14).

Time Management

First-year teachers are often overwhelmed by the amount of work that needs to be done in a day; in the beginning, they may spend up to 70 hours per week on schoolwork (Moir, 1999). Even within the school day itself, time management can be difficult. Without experience, the beginning teacher may not be able to judge how long an individual lesson or activity will take. If the project takes longer than anticipated, students may not be able to complete it. If it takes less time, the teacher may be left with the problem of unstructured chaos.

In addition to juggling the demands of the job, balancing personal and professional time can be difficult. Complaints from family members and friends, common in the first year, only compound the problems. "I thought I'd be busy, something like student teaching," one new teacher said, "but this is crazy. I'm feeling like I'm constantly running. It's hard to focus on other aspects of my life."

Still others feel as if teaching has completely taken over their lives. One pointed out that teaching is like holding three separate jobs: one during the school day (actually teaching), another in the afternoon after the students leave (attending meetings and dealing with other administrative tasks), and yet a third in the evenings and on weekends (planning and grading papers). Often the beginner finds it impossible to keep school hours within reason and ends up with work encroaching on all aspects of life. "If I only had one day off to plan for every day I teach, I'd be all right," one commented.

An Overwhelming Workload

Under the umbrella of *workload* are not only the activities that teachers must prepare, teaching assignments outside their area of expertise, and assignments to "difficult" classes but also a vast number of extracurricular responsibilities. Beginning teachers often end up with classes larger than those of experienced teachers and, in the upper grades, with a disproportionate number of remedial courses to teach. They may also be assigned to teach a variety of subjects, some of them outside of their primary interest. Extracurricular activities might include committee work, lunch duty, extra counseling, and extracurricular student activities. Paperwork alone can be overwhelming for a teacher who does not have time built into the day to take care of it and who has not anticipated all the forms to fill out. All in all, the workload of a novice could well be larger—not smaller—than that of a veteran.

Classroom Instruction

In this category are planning and carrying out instruction, as well as locating resources and materials and coping with a wide variety of student abilities in the same class. Using technology effectively and evaluating student progress are two related tasks.

Although all teachers must prepare lesson plans, veteran teachers are at least able to scaffold new concepts, strategies, and curriculum onto their previous learning, knowledge, and experience. Beginning teachers must develop all lessons from the start. Without help, many have difficulty adapting what they have learned in college courses into effective activities for students. In addition, beginning teachers at the middle or high school level often have a wider variety of subject matter to plan for than do those who have been around longer. Teachers in the San Diego study expressed particular frustration at needing to be proficient in different subject areas, sometimes in unrelated disciplines, which required the development of completely different lesson plans (Mathison, 1996, p. 12). No additional time is provided for this extra workload.

Presenting materials in ways that are both challenging and under-standable for students today is difficult. Students entering school now vary widely in their readiness to learn and come with different languages, values, and backgrounds. Working with such a diverse group is especially difficult for teachers who have not been prepared to do so (Pearson & Honig, 1992, p. 11). Assessing these students can also be difficult, again because of the wide variety of backgrounds the children bring with them to school. For more information on this topic, see "Working with Students" in Chapter 4, Beyond Survival.

Technology in the Classroom

Changes in technology have recently caused additional teacher anxiety. These problems lie both in knowing how to use the equipment with the students and in using the technology effectively for teaching methodology (Wilson, Ireton, & Wood, 1997, p. 400). Only a few years ago, computers in schools were used mainly for enrichment activities and variety or to teach students about computers (i.e., in computer literacy classes)— rarely to provide students with instruction in core academic subjects (Means, 2000, p. 188). Teachers today are expected to engage students in more authentic tasks, however, using tools identical or analogous to those that professionals in the work world employ, such as word processing, databases, spreadsheets, and PowerPoint presentations. In some schools, rather than doing math exercises or reading about science topics on a computer, students use computer tools to support their work in complex projects involving math, science, and other subject areas. Many schools have turned to word processing software to support student writing. Teachers worry about the need to keep abreast of all the latest technology. "Everything I know will be obsolete in two years!" laments one.

Teachers also are concerned with equity issues in schools and often feel frustrated that computers are found in four times as many of the nation's wealthiest schools as in the poorest schools (Means, 2000, p. 189). When computers are donated for school use, they may be outdated systems. In one situation, an urban high school was able to obtain 300 new computers for its classrooms—only to find that the computers could not be used because of inadequate electrical infrastructure. Finally, research studies indicate that even when schools serving low-income students do have computers, they tend to use the technology for drill and practice in basic skills rather than more broadly, as tools for learning.

As a twist, recent college graduates who begin teaching careers are often trained in modern computer use; they have learned to use state-of-the-art equipment more advanced than what the more experienced mentor may be familiar with. Sometimes beginning teachers have difficulty working with the older systems they find in today's schools—without the color printers, high-speed modems, and other peripherals they learned about in their pre-service training—and must adjust to the less desirable equipment. In this case, the beginning teacher may well have more training than the mentor does, but may need the advice of a mentor for adapting that knowledge to the available hardware and software. Beginning teachers and their mentors must wrestle with all of these technology issues together.

High-Stakes Accountability

Finally, assessment of students causes tension for many beginning (as well as some experienced) teachers, who wrestle with matching classroom learning objectives to assessments, with the wide variety of assessments, and with assessing standards and benchmarks. Standardized testing can cause anxiety when teachers find themselves being evaluated according to how well their students do. Teachers fear that they will be held personally responsible for students who do not do well, even when teachers do not control many of the variables leading to success on standardized tests (Wilson et al., 1997, p. 400).

Complicating matters even more is the fact that teachers and students face overlapping and competing demands from layers of assessments. Most school systems use a variety of large-scale assessments, including district assessments focused on local content standards, state tests reflecting state content standards, norm-referenced tests, and college admission exams. Their interaction greatly compounds the problems in attempting to link class-room and large-scale assessment. The expectation, although not always formally stated, is that all results show steady gains on all measures. Teachers, especially beginning teachers, become confused and frustrated. Where are they supposed to focus their efforts: on district standards or on mandatory, norm-referenced testing? Whose standards are more important: the district's or the state's? What if grade-level texts do not cover what's on the test? In this era of accountability, these are grave concerns in most faculty rooms.

Sociocultural Awareness and Sensitivity

According to the California New Teacher Project (Commission on Teacher Credentialing, 1991), beginning teachers often find themselves assigned to teach in "highly complex environments" that would challenge even a seasoned veteran—for example, in inner-city schools with high percentages of low-income, ethnolinguistically and culturally diverse children. First-year teachers may well deal with ethnic groups with whom they have never had previous contact. Effective teachers celebrate the diversity of cultures in their classrooms and strive to improve human relations among their students. Yet, beginning teachers may find it difficult to teach when they don't understand a culture within their classroom and may even fight against a fear of a group they don't understand. Attempting to communicate with parents who do not speak English only adds to the problem.

One beginning high school teacher, for example, spent many hours during his first year attempting to convince the parents of several Hispanic students that their children needed to improve their attendance. These students often missed school to help with a younger sibling, to provide transportation for a family member, or sometimes to work. The teacher soon became frustrated in his attempts to communicate with the families. He realized that part of the problem was that he did not speak Spanish and needed constantly to rely on translators, often the students themselves. Only after some time did he discover another central problem in communication, however: a difference in values. Although he had seen missing school as an expression of a lack of respect for education, he eventually realized that it had more to do with a cultural priority in favor of family. Some of the parents did not understand his concern, he realized, because they felt it was more important for the student to contribute to the family (by caring for a sibling or earning money) than to go to school. A mentor experienced in working with students from this culture might have helped him communicate better and with more understanding from the beginning.

Teachers might also have difficulty working with children who have been abused and may be uncomfortable with the legal requirement that they report a suspicion of abuse. They might work with the children of mothers who abused drugs while pregnant or with children who suffer from autism, processing problems, or attention deficit/hyperactivity disorder, for example. Children growing up in poverty or within transient families may raise unexpected issues for the first-year teacher as well. Children growing up in unconventional families—families with two mothers or those going through a heated divorce and custody battle, for example—may have special needs or sensitivities unfamiliar to the beginning teacher as well.

In the San Diego study, 13 of 15 new teachers interviewed reported extreme discomfort with ethnic friction and sexual behavior among students, and all 15 agreed that "their lack of understanding of the different social and cultural behaviors of their students made both planning and instruction very difficult" (Mathison, 1996, p. 12). Whereas diversity within the classroom can be enriching, it also adds to the layers of challenge for the beginning teacher trying to reach all students. "I knew the first year would be difficult," writes one beginning teacher, "but I didn't expect all of the pressures of dealing with at-risk students on top of the pressures of being a first-year teacher" (Pearson & Honig, 1992, p. 7).

Student Motivation

Many teachers fear that their students will not be receptive to their instruction and will refuse to learn. In fact, this fear is often valid (Wilson et al., 1997, p. 399). In the San Diego study, 6 of 15 new teachers complained that the students' lack of motivation "to do anything" was particularly demoralizing (Mathison, 1996, p. 13). The problem is compounded when it comes to students who have special needs. These students, even more than others, are often afraid to take risks and constantly fear that they will fail. Inability to motivate special-needs students and others can cause anxiety for the teacher; discussing this anxiety with a more experienced teacher may alleviate it.

A Solitary Work Environment

One of the great challenges of teaching is loneliness in the classroom and the presence of what can be, at times, an awful feeling of isolation. Teachers entering the profession have rarely thought about the fact that most instructors—at virtually all levels—are alone with students most of the school day. Once in their own classroom, they rarely have the opportunity to observe other teachers in action or to turn to another professional when a question arises. From the beginning, they are the sole professionals in their domain. Without a mentor assigned specifically to work with them, they may find themselves completely independent of all other adults in their new career.

Relationships With Parents and Colleagues

Beginning teachers often worry about meetings with parents, sometimes because they fear confrontation. These teachers may need help preparing for their first back-to-school night, open house, regular parent-teacher conferences, and special conferences called by the beginning teacher or the parents to discuss problems (Jonson, 1999a). Some who are comfortable talking before children become fearful at the idea of speaking in front of adults. Conferences can be intimidating, especially the first time (Wilson et al., 1997, p. 397). Some parents object to having their children taught by new teachers, which can put the new teacher even more on edge. Conversely, parents' lack of interest can be discouraging. When the parental conference is likely to be emotionally charged, the beginning teacher can benefit greatly from a veteran's suggestions.

Fitting in with and gaining acceptance from peers can also be a challenge. As beginning teachers learn to negotiate the social realities of the faculty room, they often butt up against the old norms of individualism, isolationism, and privatism. For a mentor-mentee relationship to be successful, mentors must be selected because they are on the cusp of change in school culture, in an ideal position to forgo individual work for joint work. They must model the values of collegiality, openness, and trust over detachment and territoriality. In so doing, they will help beginning teachers develop new ways of doing business and of viewing themselves and their profession.

CONCLUSION

Most beginning teachers find themselves in culture shock soon after starting their professional careers; often their preservice training (if they had any) has not prepared them adequately for the real challenges of their profession. Classroom management and discipline are only two of the issues of concern to these beginners. It is important for mentors to think back to their own early years and remember the issues that they worried about then.

Chapter 4 looks at the many skills required of any teacher: teaching, interpersonal, and coping skills. Just as effective mentors need to remember their early anxieties, they also need to continually refer to these basic skills.

> New teachers yearn for a sense of professional rootedness and community. Too often, however, they know only a sense of dislocation and loneliness, of compromise and inadequacy—feelings that cause them to question their commitment to school life.... Many beginning teachers find themselves in school systems that are ill-prepared to welcome them appropriately. These beginners are isolated professionally and socially. They join aging and habit-bound faculties whose members already know the ropes. They become the have-nots among the haves, the ones with neither the tricks of the trade nor with wisdom of experience (Moran, 1990, pp. 210–211).

4

Beyond Survival

Miss Jacobs, a new teacher at Central Elementary, is planning a required unit on volcanoes as part of her third-grade science curriculum.

She has three weeks to teach the unit. Miss Jacobs's favorite subject is science, and she is excited about working with her class on this unit. She still remembers an experiment she did related to the topic when she was a child, although she can't remember exactly how old she was at the time.

At Central Elementary, all third-grade teachers use a standard science textbook, which includes a unit on the topic of volcanoes. Miss Jacobs does not like the book and is particularly unenthusiastic about this chapter, but she's been told she must use it. Mr. Bennett, another third-grade teacher, has suggested that she assign supplementary reading material as well if she would like, but she's not sure that the children will do both, and she wants to leave time for activities other than reading.

In addition to assigning and discussing the reading, Miss Jacobs would like to have her students do the hands-on experiment she remembers from her childhood. Also, Mr. Bennett has just told her that the local public library, within walking distance, has a special exhibit on volcanoes. He has suggested that she mention it to her students in case any of them would like to go see it after school someday. She wonders out loud why the two classes can't go on a field trip to see the exhibit. Mr. Bennett agrees that the students might learn a lot from the experience, but says he doesn't have time to coordinate it. Miss Jacobs volunteers to organize it and make plans for both classes.

Miss Jacobs has two students in her classroom with learning disabilities and one who is pulled out for speech class on Tuesdays and Thursdays. Three of her students struggle with their reading and often need help with textbook assignments. She also has a student in the gifted program and another who seems to have an exceptional aptitude for science. She has already arranged with the librarian for the field trip and okayed the date with Mr. Bennett when she passes the speech teacher in the hall and realizes suddenly that the scheduled date will conflict with speech pullout.

Miss Jacobs has 20 students in her class and a small, portable classroom with little extra space. Desks are currently arranged in rows, facing the front. For the science experiment she has planned, students will need to work together in groups of four on a project that will require a large amount of space. Furthermore, one phase of the project, involving papier mâché, will need to dry overnight, so the space will need to be designated for a few days.

Miss Jacobs wants to start the unit with a discussion, followed by in-class reading time. But the students read at different paces, so she must be sure to have something to occupy the fast readers. She also knows from previous projects that her gifted student has great ideas but tends to irritate some of the other children when working in small groups because she doesn't like to listen to their ideas. Most of the kids have difficulty beginning a project in small groups, and several will need constant supervision if they are to remain on task.

Because it is flu season in her community, absenteeism at Central Elementary is high. Miss Jacobs fills out daily attendance records, but she also needs to keep close track of who has been at school for what part of the science project so she can make sure those who are ill can somehow make up the work and gain the understanding they need in time for later parts of the project. Because she has decided to base much of their grade on student participation in conducting the experiment, she needs to have a way to monitor that participation and provide makeup opportunities.

Miss Jacobs is pleased to find a six-page article in a children's magazine, including lots of color illustrations, that covers most of the same information about volcanoes as the textbook but in a more interesting way; she can supplement this material with discussion, she thinks. Mr. Bennett insists that she must use the standard text, however. She wonders if he's right about this but doesn't want to offend him by questioning too much. Also, she doesn't know if she can photocopy the pages to give to the students. If she can, she'll need to ask about the procedure. If not, she'll need to figure out a way for everyone to read the original.

She also needs to find out about school policies regarding field trips.

Permission slips go home with the children, and she sends out interest forms to all the parents in her class and in Mr. Bennett's class to find chaperones. When the forms come back, she finds that she is one adult short of the required ratio. In addition, she vaguely remembers that a second-grade teacher has warned her not to allow one of her parent volunteers, Mr. Smith, to have sole responsibility for any of the kids. She can't remember why not or who told her or even for certain if Mr. Smith is the correct person.

On a trial walk to the library, Miss Jacobs realizes that the group will need to cross two very busy streets en route. She wants to telephone a few parents to ask them directly if they could possibly help chaperone the field trip, but she doesn't know any of them and doesn't want to put anyone on the spot. She wonders if she should talk with Mr. Smith in particular about watching the kids closely, especially considering she won't have any extra adults, but she doesn't want to seem mistrusting. She wishes she could remember who warned her about Mr. Smith and what the problem was.

She also wishes that Mr. Bennett would help her more with planning this field trip and finds herself becoming short-tempered with him, though she reminds herself that she did volunteer. She is just wondering if she should cancel the trip when she finds a note from Mr. Bennett saying that one of his parents has volunteered late to go along, so the trip is legal, and he's looking forward to it. The day before the volcano project is to begin, Miss Jacobs gives away tickets she has to a concert that night and works long hours preparing so she will be ready for the unit.

The next morning, she is eager to begin but also somewhat discouraged. Despite her good intentions, she never did talk to anyone about the textbook and ends up assigning the reading from it despite her wishes. As she predicted, some of the kids are uninterested and spend their reading time talking with each other and drawing pictures in their notebooks. When she reminds them to get back to work, one informs her that the book is boring.

The night before the field trip, she can't sleep. She has met her legal quota for chaperones, but she wonders if she should have gotten extra adults given the busy street crossings and Mr. Smith's shaky record.

Miss Jacobs wishes the project were over. She should have followed the suggestions of the other third-grade teachers, she thinks, and just had the kids read and answer questions. She hopes the kids will be excited about the experiment, but she no longer has faith that they will be. She hopes it won't be too hard for them and wishes she had thought more about that beforehand. Perhaps she should have left an extra half-hour to work on it. But then they would be late to music class.

She thinks maybe she'll do something easier for the next unit.

While much of designing a lesson may be second nature for the experienced teacher, the process is not so natural for the novice. Even the beginning teacher with original and creative ideas, like Miss Jacobs, may have difficulty fitting all the pieces together to maximize learning for the variety of students in the classroom. In addition to drawing from teaching skills, the teacher must use a variety of interpersonal skills to enlist the help of others at the school and perhaps to solicit parent involvement. A beginning teacher may well need assistance juggling everything to keep from becoming discouraged.

Thus, an effective mentor should not only understand the fears of a beginning teacher but also review the basics of teaching required at all levels of experience and be prepared to assist the mentee with suggestions and support. A good mentor should be aware of the mentee's skills, attempt to help the beginning teacher develop proficiency, and provide encouragement when things do not seem to be working.

The beginning teacher needs support in developing three categories of required abilities: *teaching skills* (planning lessons, working with students, managing the classroom, and dealing with administrative tasks); *interpersonal skills* (working with colleagues and other school personnel, dealing with parents, adhering to school policy, and supporting the school and the district); and *coping skills* (balancing work time with personal time, learning from colleagues, managing stress, and continuing professional development). To progress from the early phases of survival to the level of professional, the teacher must develop all of these skills while increasing knowledge of both content and pedagogy.

TEACHING SKILLS

Of all the skills required, the basics of teaching are most likely to have been covered thoroughly in preservice credential courses. Even so, beginning teachers may have difficulty putting theory to practice in the classroom and adapting what they have learned to their specific situations. Both the variety of students at a particular work site and the policies of the system could affect outcome, even with the most careful preparation. Miss Jacobs, for example, had to draw on a wide variety of teaching skills to plan her lessons for the unit on volcanoes. She needed to figure out how to work with students of varying abilities in her classroom, how to set up the classroom so that the experiment could be done successfully, and how to assess her students' learning. Administrative tasks for this unit included obtaining permission slips and chaperones for the field trip.

Lesson Planning

Effective teaching depends on effective lesson planning. To maximize both student learning and appropriate classroom behavior, teachers must thoughtfully and carefully prepare for every minute with the students. This task can be overwhelming for the beginner. Whereas a seasoned teacher can draw from past experience and adapt previously prepared lessons, the beginning teacher must develop everything from the start. The veteran teacher has an idea about what will and what won't work, but the novice has only theory to work with.

Developing strategies for effective teaching is a continuous process, with an ongoing learning curve for all teachers. Throughout this process, the teacher must link curriculum, specific instruction, and assessment to standards-based learning. To be effective, the teacher needs to be able to do the following:

1. Develop instructional strategies and methods.
   a. Cover essential core curriculum over the course of the year.
   b. Schedule each day and week to address all subject areas within the given time frames.
   c. Plan daily lessons and thematic units.
   d. Constantly align lesson objectives with standards to be addressed.
   e. Maximize time spent on learning.

2. Select curriculum materials, again keeping standards in mind at all times.

3. Perform assessments (formative, diagnostic, summative, formal, and informal).

Developing Instructional Strategies. A mentor can help the beginning teacher keep in mind the primary goals of lesson planning: to maximize time spent on academic subjects and to manage the classroom so that students are engaged, on task, and achieving success. To accomplish these goals, the teacher needs to motivate students by keeping the lessons interesting. In addition, the teacher needs to continually relate instruction to standards. The Unit Planning Form in Figure 4.1 might help a new teacher in planning instruction.

If a beginning teacher is struggling with a unit or complains that students are not interested, a mentor should consider whether that teacher is using a variety of strategies for teaching. The mentor could suggest different techniques for getting a point across and perhaps suggest alternative activities to help the beginning teacher think about a strategy that might be more effective (see Box 4.1). By brainstorming together, the two might come up with a lesson that deals with the curriculum but that is more interesting and effective.

Figure 4.1   Unit planning form

   I. Duration (dates and times): _____

  II. Students (grade level): _____

      Student Characteristics:

      _____

      _____

 III. Unit Topic or Theme: _____

 IV. Subjects: _____

  V. Unit Objectives (incorporate required standards): _____

      _____

      _____

      _____

 VI. Materials and Media (curriculum books, materials, and resources
      to be used): _____

      _____

      _____

      _____

      _____

VII. Procedures/Instructional Activities

      A. Introduction (procedure for introducing the unit): _____

          _____

          _____

          _____

B. Content and Activities (at least six lesson topics, with preliminary notes on content, teaching strategies, activities, and assignments for each): _____

_____

_____

_____

_____

_____

_____

_____

_____

_____

C. Culminating Activity: _____

_____

_____

_____

_____

VIII. Evaluation (indicators for success, procedure[s] for assessment of learner understanding): _____

_____

_____

_____

_____

_____

SOURCE: Adapted from Jonson (1997).

BOX 4.1

Activities to Use for Instruction

- Instructing the entire class
- Leading whole-class discussions
- Organizing small-group discussions
- Having students do activities in small groups
- Arranging for a resource person to visit
- Allowing time for students to work independently on projects
- Having students write in journals
- Going on a field trip
- Listening to tapes
- Making models
- Making charts, diagrams, posters, maps, or graphs
- Having students give oral reports
- Telling stories
- Having students dramatize or role-play
- Playing instructional games
- Making bulletin boards
- Making displays
- Viewing films, videos, or slides
- Having students do library research
- Having a panel discussion
- Having demonstrations
- Having students sing or perform finger plays
- Encouraging high-level thinking through specific questions
- Using hands-on engaged student learning
- Using cooperative learning strategies, such as jigsaw puzzles or a team games tournament
- Using problem-based learning
- Using technology for Internet research, keypals, and other online learning projects
- Using teacher-made graphic organizers or having students make their own graphic organizers
- Using reciprocal teaching
- Using differentiated assignments
- Using inductive teaching strategies, such as concept attainment
- Using scaffolding prior to assigning silent reading for students who don't quite "get it"

One critical problem many beginning teachers (and some veterans) have is identifying what they want students to know and be able to do and determining how they will know that students have learned it. With this in mind, the mentor can help the beginning teacher plan lessons, assess student learning, find ways to provide enrichment for those students who have mastered the concept, and find ways to provide supplementation for those who don't "get it." On the other hand, a teacher such as Miss Jacobs, who already has good ideas, may simply need encouragement and help with logistics—or she might benefit from suggestions for additional activities. A more experienced teacher might suggest that Miss Jacobs have students write in their journals, for example, to help them think about what they are learning. This could also serve as a tool for Miss Jacobs to use in tracking student progress.

Beginning teachers are often at a disadvantage in that they lack a supply of materials to select from to reinforce coursework. A veteran teacher has likely built a collection through the years of colorful posters to enliven the room and supplement lessons, books to stock a classroom library, and other supplies. Sharing surplus materials can go a long way toward enhancing the beginning teacher's curriculum. A mentor who does not have materials suitable for the mentee may know of another teacher who does. Suggesting read-aloud books or supplementary reading materials that have proven popular with students through the years can also be a big help (see Box 4.2). Offering tips for building book collections—perhaps through dividends from commercial book club orders, for example— would be another good service to the beginning teacher. Suggesting online resources—Web sites, Listservs, chat groups, and newsletters—would be helpful as well.

BOX 4.2

2,700 Good Books to Read

In July 2001, the California State Department of Education posted on the Internet an updated list of recommended works of fiction, nonfiction, poetry, and drama for kindergarten through Grade 12. The comprehensive index replaces versions released in 1990 and 1996 and can be accessed by various search categories, including grade level, genre, and language. There are titles in English, Spanish, Hmong, Vietnamese, Chinese, and Filipino/Tagalog. Synopses are included in annotations, which may also suggest links to a particular state reading standard or mention what the department calls "sensitive subject matter." Go to http://www.cde.ca.gov.

Developing Assessment Tools and Techniques. Teachers have many options for assessing student progress and achievement, some formal and others informal. Some forms of assessment relate specifically to the particular classroom and are in the hands of the teacher. The goal of classroom assessment is not only to determine the student's ability to perform in a given subject area but also to monitor and adjust teaching. These assessments might be based on culminating exhibitions or presentations, writing samples, portfolios (collections of work showing development in progress), classroom observations over a period of time, questionnaires and surveys, or oral questions and interviews.

Good mentors can help beginning teachers by sharing techniques commonly used at their school and by discussing school policies about assessment. The mentor can also make sure that the beginning teacher has a procedure in place for evaluating and determining grades. The beginning teacher might even benefit from a general discussion about the purposes of assessment: to obtain information on student progress to report to parents, to learn where instructional planning needs improvement, and to make students aware of their strengths.

One of the most formal types of assessment, the commercial standardized test, is usually required of all children in a given system. Beginning teachers need to understand what is on these tests, how they are to be administered, and what to communicate about them to parents or older students. They need to understand the purposes of standardized testing and to be able to analyze the data from these tests. After analysis, a mentor may be able to assist the beginning teacher in planning instruction that will help individuals who lack skills or in planning extensions for enrichment of students who score high on the tests. Even on a logistical level, beginning teachers or teachers new to a district may need help with assessment timelines and procedures for district- or state-mandated assessments. Mentors can make sure that these new teachers understand the requirements, procedures, and conditions of testing.

Working With Students

A skilled teacher reaches all students, from struggling and special needs students to gifted learners. As in Miss Jacobs's case, a class may include students who need to be pulled out at times for a variety of reasons—from speech therapy to remedial reading—as well as some who need special attention within the classroom (because they have trouble learning or because they learn quickly and require enrichment). An effective teacher will do the following:

1. Address the individual needs of individual students
   a. Assess resources for students
   b. Allow for specialists and pullout classes
   c. Assist a child who has been pulled out or absent in re-entering the classroom afterward

2. Motivate and engage students in active learning

Addressing individual needs includes, in particular, adapting for students with special needs and learning difficulties and working with English Language Learners.

Addressing Individual Needs. Good teachers respect all students and treat all fairly. In addition, they work with individuals regardless of their special needs. A mentor can help the beginning teacher learn about resources available within the school to help with special needs and about school policy regarding pullout students. Through observation and experience, a mentor may also help beginning teachers become aware of individual students needing extra assistance. Without experience, the beginning teacher may fail to recognize that some students are struggling because they *can't* understand the lesson, rather than because they are not trying.

Gifted children also often need special attention. A teacher must learn to recognize and meet the needs of a gifted student who has shut down and is not performing. The teacher must recognize that a child who is gifted in one area may not be gifted in another. A mentor can help the beginning teacher know where to go in the school system for additional help with resources or testing for gifted children or simply to consult with an expert.

Adapting for Students with Special Needs and Learning Difficulties. Often one of the biggest challenges that mentors and new teachers face is how to make adaptations for mainstreamed special education students. Mentor, teacher, and parents may need to work together to maximize the learning potential of the special needs student and to create a positive, productive, and successful classroom community for all. Often, new teachers find that their special needs students require a great deal of their attention. They struggle to meet the needs of both the general class population and the special needs student. Mainstreamed students with physical disabilities may not require much additional attention. But if their special need students come with emotional disabilities, autistic spectrum diagnosis, or behavioral disabilities, the teaching situation can rapidly become difficult. For example, a new teacher in a first-grade classroom may need to interrupt a read-aloud many times to address the behavioral needs of an emotionally challenged student who is disruptive, having difficulty focusing, and having emotional outbursts.

A child with special needs may require transition from a regular classroom to the special needs classroom and may be shadowed by an educational assistant throughout the day. The curriculum for the special needs child is usually planned by a collaborative team of teachers, parents, and paraprofessionals and adapted to fit individual needs. The mentor often needs to help the new teacher work with the paraprofessional(s) and interpret the Individual Education Plan (IEP).

Outlined here are a few useful strategies to assist special needs students who struggle with learning or demonstrate some difficulty with everyday classroom tasks.

- Break work into small chunks so that the student can achieve a small amount of success each day. For some students, large assignments can seem daunting and unattainable.

- If the student has difficulty copying notes from the board or over-head projector, offer an alternative so that the work can still be done. For example, make a photocopy of the overhead transparency for the student to use.
- Minimize disruptions by placing the student in a seat away from the temptation of excess chatting, other noise, high-traffic areas, or distractions such as windows.
- For students who require constant reminders about how to follow class procedures, provide a checklist of the daily routine or assignment expectations to be taped to the student's desk or binder. This will enable the student to keep track of work more independently.
- Reserve a daily morning time for checking student planners and homework so that expectations are clear and students can clear up any difficulties right away and still work toward achieving a productive day.
- Review the student's IEP and follow through with recommended learning adaptations set by the school or a former teacher.

Working With English Language Learners. According to the 2000 census, 47 million people (18% of the population) in the United States speak a language other than English at home. By 2030, this percentage will increase to 40%. As the number of English Language Learners (ELLs) has increased, the politics of English language learning has become both more prominent and complicated. Issues such as funding for bilingual education and English as a Second Language (ESL) programs, the pros and cons of making English the official language of the United States, and the status of ELL students in the context of testing are all sites of contested views. In the midst of the politics, legislative proposals, and policy statements on the issue, new teachers are often faced daily with the challenges of English language learning in the mainstream classroom (NCTE ELL Task Force, 2006).

Knowledge of students is key to good teaching. The mentor and new teacher may find it worthwhile to explore how the ELL students differ in various ways, including their level of oral English proficiency, literacy ability in both the heritage language and English, and cultural backgrounds. If the new teacher's ELLs are born in the United States, they may have developed conversational language abilities in English but lack academic language proficiency. Newcomers, on the other hand, need to develop both conversational and academic English. Education gained before entering U.S. schools helps determine students' literacy levels in their native language. Some ELLs may have age- and grade-level skills, whereas others have limited or no literacy because of the quality of previous schooling, interrupted schooling due to wars or migration, and other circumstances (Suárez-Orozco & Suárez-Orozco, 2001). Given the wide range of ELLs and their backgrounds, it is important that new teachers take the time to learn about their students, particularly their literacy histories.

Second language learners need to develop academic proficiency in English to master content-area subjects. Mentors can assist new teachers in providing effective instruction for these students by helping the mentee do the following:

- Provide authentic opportunities for ELL students to use language in a nonthreatening environment
- Teach key vocabulary connected with the topic of the lesson
- Teach academic oral language in the context of various content areas
- Teach text- and sentence-level grammar in context to help students understand the structure and style of the English language
- Teach the specific features of language that students need to communicate in social as well as academic contexts
- Recognize that second language acquisition is a gradual developmental process and is built on students' knowledge and skill in their native language

Motivating Students. Most teachers have an ongoing concern regarding student motivation. If students are not motivated to learn, classroom management becomes a problem, and valuable lesson time is lost to discipline. If students *are* motivated, time on task increases, and learning improves.

Students will want to learn if the curriculum is interesting and the classroom enjoyable. They will rise to a lesson that is challenging and for which a variety of activities have been planned and a variety of materials introduced. A positive, personable teacher will also inspire students, and providing occasional rewards can be well worth the investment. A student who feels comfortable with the learning situation is most likely to feel free to learn, grow, and change.

Here again, the mentor can help by suggesting to the beginning teacher ways to keep a lesson varied and exciting and an environment pleasant. An observant mentor may be able to see whether the classroom is encouraging to the students and, if not, to offer suggestions for improvement. The mentor might also want to help the beginning teacher concerned about lack of student motivation to evaluate the classroom. Together, the two could review and reflect on the following questions:

- Is the room physically attractive and inviting to students? Are interest centers, bulletin boards, students' desks, tables, and furniture arranged in a pleasant manner that is conducive to learning? Are books, learning materials, wall displays, pictures, and charts interesting, and are they changed regularly? Might a plant or a small pet make the room more inviting?
- Are students involved in decision making? Do they get to make choices regarding daily routine, themes, or topics of study?

- Are students encouraged to participate in a range of activities and projects? Are lessons appropriate for multiple intelligences and learning modalities?
- Are students who finish assignments early kept challenged and given the opportunity to work on additional activities, such as special projects, computer practice, free reading, and so on? Are these projects meaningful and not simply designed to keep the quick achiever busy?
- Is student work displayed throughout the room? Is it changed regularly? Do students feel successful and proud of their work?
- Are students praised for their efforts and sometimes rewarded? Are parents and other students notified of exceptional work?
- Are students encouraged routinely with smiles or kind words? Are they listened to? Complimented?
- Are students asked questions about their interests and experiences? Do they know the teacher cares?
- Do students understand why they are learning the material?

Students learn best when they feel they are in a safe, accepting environment. Evaluating the classroom setting and atmosphere can help the beginning teacher provide such an environment.

Classroom Management

The distance between theory and reality is greater when it comes to classroom management than for any other single area of teaching. New teachers often find themselves ill prepared for this aspect of the profession and are shocked at the difficulties they encounter when they start their first professional assignment. Managing the class effectively can sometimes seem impossible. The goals in this area are the following:

1. Organize the physical space of the classroom

2. Provide a safe and orderly learning environment

3. Establish effective classroom discipline systems

Organizing Physical Space. Because teaching style affects seating plans, every teacher must give careful thought to where and how students are seated in the classroom. Are they to be at individual desks in rows, or in table groups? Will the children be working often in small groups—or will they most often work individually or as a large group? If they are seated in groups, are the groups arranged at random, or do children choose where to sit? Will the teacher mix them by ability? Or divide them by ability? How many children to a group? Do some children need to be closer to the front of the classroom so they can hear or see well? Do certain children need a supportive friend nearby to bring out their best? Must other children be separated from friends with whom they might chatter? Where can a child sit who has difficulty working in close proximity to others? Frequent changes in group assignments encourage students to work with and get to know a broader range of children and allow for problems to be worked out through the year.

In addition to the placement of student desks, other aspects of the physical arrangement of the classroom must be addressed. Where is the teacher to sit? Is the teacher's desk easily accessible? Is there a central meeting place in the room as well—especially for younger children? If so, can the children sit comfortably, positioned so that all can see and hear each other? Lack of attention in group activities could be caused by the children's inability to participate fully, not by their lack of interest. Is a black- or whiteboard nearby? Can a chart or a sample be positioned within view of every child?

Where will items be stored in the classroom? Where is the pencil sharpener? A classroom library? Is the library inviting? Will children want to go there in their free time? How will bulletin boards be used?

All of these things will affect the way students learn and their comfort within the classroom. Especially if space is limited, it might take some experimenting to establish the setting most conducive to learning.

Providing a Safe and Orderly Learning Environment. Children like a predictable environment, a consistent classroom with dependable routines. At the elementary school level, a morning routine allows children to start their day comfortably and should include an agenda for activities planned throughout the day. Morning rituals might include a song, a reading, journal writing, or other age-appropriate activities. For secondary students, a routine at the beginning of each period helps keep them on track. The secondary teacher might begin each period by collecting and reviewing homework, answering questions, or having students write in journals or read quietly, for example. A veteran teacher is sure to have other grade-appropriate suggestions as well.

Classroom management style varies from teacher to teacher, depending on personality and individual preferences, the age group of the students, and, with older groups, the subject matter. Some teachers conduct mostly teacher-led whole-class instruction and discussions, whereas others rely more on small-group activities. Some tolerate less noise than others, some require more order than others, and so on.

Beginning teachers must establish any class routines, rules, and procedures they choose to implement during the first few days of school. Many teachers enlist the help of their students to set "the rules" and then post them throughout the year; others come the first day with predetermined guidelines. Depending on the age group, rules could be as simple as "Try your best" or "Organize your space." One secondary teacher states simply, "Act appropriately"—and spends a good half-hour at the beginning of the year discussing the word *appropriately*. Signals for quiet should be clear to the students from the beginning. Clapping hands, whispering directions, or turning out the lights are only a few of the techniques teachers use to signal silence. Routines should be spelled out, whether they regard speaking during discussions, using the restroom, or turning in homework. Explaining to students why rules are necessary might help with later enforcement. A mentor can help with specific details about school-wide rules and policies.

Establishing Effective Classroom Discipline Systems. Experienced teachers are more likely to mention classroom management and discipline as their most difficult problems during their first years of teaching than anything else. Even in classrooms where students are generally well behaved, occasional problems arise. Through the years, effective teachers develop strategies for dealing with problems, but beginning teachers may struggle for some time as they search to find what works for them.

Consequences for breaking the class rules should be clear to students from the beginning, just as the rules themselves should be clear from Week 1. Consequences work best if they are explained ahead of time and are specific and appropriate for the action. A mentor can help the beginning teacher make sure that the consequences are in line with school policies. Are time-outs in the hallway acceptable? Can students be kept in at recess or after school?

The most effective discipline is logical and appropriate. Children who run should go back where they started from and walk, for example. Children who write on desks should clean all the desks during recess. A secondary student might be required to serve detention after school following tardiness or might have to attend study hall to make up missing assignments. Time-outs may well provide an opportunity for misbehaving children to think about their actions and decide to behave appropriately. Again, a detention for a secondary student may serve the same purpose.

A mentor can help a beginning teacher see when consequences are working and when they are not. If students are misbehaving, examination of classroom management and curriculum may reveal the solution. If rules are not clear enough, they may need to be changed or clarified.

With experience, the teacher learns not only to handle problems effectively but also to prevent them in the first place; preventing a problem is always better than dealing with it after it occurs. If students are not on task, perhaps the activities are too simple or too difficult. Maybe a different seating arrangement would work better. Sometimes an experienced colleague is just the person to look objectively at a situation and help the flustered novice gain the perspective to deal with a situation appropriately.

Administrative Tasks

Even veteran teachers often struggle to find time for the huge amounts of paperwork that come across their desks. For a novice, the piles can be overwhelming. The sheer amount is one problem; understanding all the forms is another. In addition to the actual teaching, teachers are responsible for the following tasks:

1. Keeping records

2. Grading

3. Understanding and following school policies and procedures

Paperwork falls roughly into two categories: (1) teaching related (class plans, records of student accomplishment, assessment tools, and so on) and (2) nonteaching related (forms related to school and district policies, attendance sheets, memos, meeting agendas and minutes, and so on). Researchers at the Beginning Teacher Evaluation Study, conducted by Far West Laboratory, found that elementary teachers devoted 60% of their day to academic activities, 23% to nonacademic activities, and 17% to non-instructional activities.

Keeping Records. Relying on memory when it comes time to produce report cards can be extremely dangerous. Although a teacher might expect to remember some details of a student's progress and achievement, the specifics often vanish when it comes time to assign a grade. Students blur, activities blur, and what seemed clear when it happened is very unclear after time has passed. Careful record keeping will help the teacher make insightful comments and will be useful if a student or parent challenges a grade.

Although paperwork in education is often viewed as burdensome, it has value and cannot be eliminated. Teachers can use a variety of strategies to handle paperwork more effectively and efficiently. A mentor can help the new teacher survive the "paper snowstorm" by sharing time-saving tips and demonstrating record-keeping strategies, including grade book organization, curriculum-based assessment tracking, and monitoring of student progress, observational notes, parent/conference records, student portfolios, and so on. Many veteran teachers stay organized with a liberal use of sticky notes, putting them on the tops of forms, student schedules, work samples and anecdotal records, classroom schedules and arrangements, standardized testing schedules, preholiday days, and so forth.

New teachers report often feeling lost, unorganized, and unsure of what they were doing their first time through a year of record keeping. The second year is much easier. With experience, new teachers develop their own system, which they continue to use and refine. So it gets easier. Good advice is to expect record keeping to be tough the first year. Once mentees make it through just once, they'll know that they can do it every time.

Grading. If records have been kept carefully and ongoing assessments performed, grading will be much easier than if these preliminary steps have not been carried out. Still, a beginning teacher may struggle, especially with students whose work is inconsistent. When comments are written along with grades on report cards or papers, a "second set of eyes" can raise important questions of logic or tone. Does the comment make sense? Is its meaning clear? Is it written in a way that will be constructive and not offensive?

Beginning teachers may need to be reminded that a written comment is permanent and must always be well thought out and carefully worded.

Following School Policies. Understanding school policies is absolutely essential for any teacher. Policies govern everything from discipline to assessment to field trips to working with special needs students. Even attendance taking can become a beginning teacher's nightmare, with specific forms required each day. In addition, middle and high school teachers must participate in house/team meetings and shared responsibilities, work with department heads and the rest of the department, and so on.

A beginner may not always know where to turn with policy questions or even when a specific policy might apply. Miss Jacobs was unsure of textbook requirements for her unit, for example, and also needed to find out the requirements for leading a field trip. A veteran teacher is often able to answer such questions easily, advising the novice when a policy might be in question or finding someone else who can help.

INTERPERSONAL SKILLS

Fitting in with the school and district culture can be a challenge for the beginning teacher. Often the teacher is new to the community as well as to the faculty and needs to build a network of people to work with. Among the interpersonal skills required at the start are the following:

1. Building collegiality with teaching peers
2. Establishing good working relationships with other staff
3. Creating a partnership with parents
   a. Communicating
   b. Conferencing
4. Understanding and carrying out the school philosophy
5. Working on school and district projects without becoming overwhelmed

In setting up her unit on volcanoes, for example, Miss Jacobs needed to work with her peer, Mr. Bennett; to schedule around the speech therapist and art teacher; and to work with parents who might chaperone the field trip. All of these tasks required interpersonal skills.

Colleagues

Gaining acceptance in a new school can take time—for the seasoned teacher new to the school as well as for a teacher just beginning in the profession. A mentor can introduce the new teacher to peers, encouraging contact with those who are positive and helpful and steering away from those likely to be more negative. Miss Jacobs, for example, needed to know where to turn to find answers about school policies regarding textbooks and copying and wasn't sure that Mr. Bennett's advice was accurate. A mentor might have been able to answer her questions or at least to get the help of someone who could. A mentor might also invite a beginning teacher to teacher social hours, union meetings, classes or workshops offered by the district, or other district grade-level networking opportunities. A new teacher who becomes acquainted with more seasoned veterans benefits not only by becoming more comfortable with the work setting but also through informal dialogue with experienced teachers.

Other School Staff

The principal, secretaries, custodial staff, volunteers, teacher aides, and resource specialists are all part of the school network. Communicating with these people is essential to varying degrees, and getting along with them can only make the teacher's job easier. A mentor can introduce the new teacher to these people and point out quirks and issues of concern to them. For example, how do custodians like the room to look at the end of the day? Who deals with spills or with necessary repairs? What teacher aides might be available in the school? What about resource specialists? How does one obtain help from them?

Parents

Parents of the students in a classroom can either support or undermine a new teacher; they can be a great help as volunteers in the classroom and can give insight into their children, or they can create tension by hovering and criticizing. Some may be indifferent, hostile, or even belligerent. Knowing this, many new teachers worry about parents or even feel threatened by the parent community. Many other parents are interested, cooperative, and supportive, however. Even most parents who appear critical only want the best for their children. It is important to remember that parents and teachers are working toward the same goal: quality education for their children.

A mentor can discuss with the beginning teacher how other teachers in the school develop partnerships with parents. How do they get parents involved? In what ways can parent volunteers help? Does the school have an established volunteer program, or does the teacher solicit help independently? Teachers new to the community as well as to the school may need to spend time getting to know the region so that they can better understand the parents. What are the backgrounds and values of the families in the community? What ethnic and cultural groups are represented? What is the economic base?

Communicating. Every teacher needs to make the effort to communicate with parents, to draw them into the program as allies from the beginning.

The beginning teacher has no grace period in acquiring this skill; parents expect professional communications from the novice just as from the veteran. In some cases, a translator may even be required to help communicate with non-English-speaking parents.

A carefully worded letter sent home on the first day of school can go a long way toward building parent-teacher relationships (see Figures 4.2 and 4.3). A mentor can help with wording that is appropriate for the specific community and age group and can also help with proofreading. It is very important that this introductory letter, as well as all other communications, be professional. If the teacher is working with children of parents who do not speak English, the help of a translator will be necessary. In some cases, especially among some cultural groups, parent response might be better if a phone call is made rather than a letter sent. Again, the help of a translator might be necessary, and a mentor might have suggestions for resources in this area. More personal notes, phone calls, e-mails, weekly newsletters, back-to-school night, open houses, and conferences provide other means of and opportunities for communication.

Figure 4.2   Sample letter home to parents (elementary school level)

[Date]

Dear Parents,

I'm excited to be starting this school year at [school name], and I look forward to sharing a successful year with your child. [Level] grade has many new and exciting experiences in store. Together we can share in the growth and development of your child.

It would be helpful if your child could bring the following items to school: [list items] Please clearly mark your child's name on all clothes, supplies, and personal items.

If at any time you have questions or concerns, feel free to contact me.

Also, let me know if you could help out on occasion with special activities, field trips, or [other].

I look forward to meeting you at our Back-to-School Night on [date]. If you need to contact me before that time, send a note or contact me at [phone number] [when] or by e-mail [give address].

Sincerely,

[Teacher]

Figure 4.3   Sample letter home to parents (middle school level)

[Date]

Dear Parents,

My name is [name], and I will be your child's [subject] teacher this year.

I'm writing not only to introduce myself, but to welcome you to the [school name] family. I am a new teacher in the [name] School District who has recently graduated from [university]. I studied [subject area] and am interested in teaching students about [state what].

I've attached a general information sheet for you and your child to read.

If you have any questions or comments about it, please note them when you sign the tear-off portion. I'll be happy to meet with you in person, talk with you on the phone, or correspond by e-mail. Generally, I will be available [state time], or you may reach me at [give phone number] or [give e-mail address].

I have many ideas for projects and activities. [State a few.] Some of them will require help. I hope that some of you will have time to work with us in planning and carrying them out. I look forward to working with you so that together we can help your child have a happy, successful time in [school name].

Sincerely,

[Teacher]

NOTE: On the general information sheet, include information on your classroom rules and expectations, grading policy, and homework requirements.

Figure 4.4   Sample form for fall conference notes (elementary school level)

Child's name: _____

Persons attending conference: _____

Date: _____

Student's adjustment to _____ grade: _____

_____

_____

_____

_____

_____

Student's achievement relative to district standards in

    Reading: _____

    Writing: _____

    Math: _____

    Social Studies: _____

    Science: _____

    Art, PE, Computer, Music (as appropriate): _____

Interaction with peers: _____

Interaction with adults: _____

Favorite friends: _____

Greatest strength: _____

Area needing most support: _____

Follow-up: _____

_____

_____

A request for parents to write about their child shows interest in hearing from them and may provide valuable information to the teacher. Questions to ask might be designed to find out what the parents would like the teacher to know about their child, how the child spends time at home, and what the parents expect of their child.

Conferencing. The parent-teacher conference is the most common means of sharing information between school and home. Careful preparation for the conference will make it go more smoothly. The mentor should encourage the new teacher to write observation notes in the weeks preceding the conference, perhaps filling out a form such as that in Figure 4.4.

When preparing for this first conference, the novice teacher should be reminded of the purposes of the conference: (a) to get information, (b) to give information, (c) to joint problem-solve, (d) to develop mutual trust, and (e) to set goals. The tone should be positive and the schedule adhered to. Mentor modeling or role playing could help things go smoothly. Discussing problem children in advance—before going to a parent with the issue—could also be very important. In addition, the mentor might suggest ways for the beginning teacher to partner with parents, such as asking parents for information about their child's learning styles and interests, areas that are difficult for the child, suggestions about handling the child's behavior, and so on. In secondary schools, the mentor could work with the beginning teacher to prepare for student-led conferences.

School Philosophy

Most schools today have developed a philosophy or vision statement that is worth reviewing and discussing. Both beginning teachers and teachers new to a district need to think about their personal fit with the school's philosophy and goals. This issue has grown in importance as social changes have altered the landscape of classrooms. Will the new teacher be able to work with the school's diverse population of students and parents? Will the new teacher devote the necessary time and energy to planning and working with colleagues to provide the best opportunity available for students? Can the new teacher provide an unwavering commitment to fully include *all* students; to recognize and respond to individual differences in students; to implement a variety of teaching strategies that result in high student achievement; to work cooperatively with parents, colleagues, support staff, and supervisors; and to display genuine respect for all? The school's philosophy will often make statements about such issues. New teachers must keep in mind the importance of the match between the vision of the school where they have accepted employment and their own vision of what it is they want to accomplish for children in the years ahead.

In addition, the teacher new to a school—whether a beginning teacher or a veteran—needs to be aware of specific goals in that school and be willing to work toward them. If the school has determined that all students should be at a certain level in reading by a certain grade, for example, the teacher needs to be aware of that goal and to be willing to commit to it.

School and District Projects

Schools and districts need teachers to commit time and energy to a wide variety of projects. These include working toward school improvement goals, serving on committees, taking part in extracurricular activities, and so forth. Offering to help with such school-wide projects is a good way for a new teacher to gain acceptance in the community—but only within limits. Overextending will only add to the frustration when daily routine itself seems too much. A good compromise would be for the new teacher to choose and become involved with one significant project. By contributing to this one project, the new teacher will prove an interest in supporting the school as a whole and will have the opportunity to network with others without sacrificing too much classroom and personal time.

COPING SKILLS

Striking a balance between professional and personal time can be difficult and may even seem impossible at first. As Miss Jacobs discovered, an ambitious class project may well mean extra hours long into the night at home. Frustrations can also add to the stress. Miss Jacobs, for example, became discouraged at the lack of help she got from Mr. Bennett.

Although enthusiastic new teachers may eagerly make sacrifices in the beginning, they will soon wear out if their time commitments are not kept in check. Mentors can suggest or teach coping skills to help the beginning teacher manage better and more efficiently or can suggest workshops to help their protégés improve skills.

Miss Jacobs approached her unit on volcanoes with many ideas and a lot of enthusiasm. As the planning proceeded and she got bogged down in details, however, she began to lose her spirit. An effective mentor would have been able to help her with her questions. In some cases, her worries were about things that could have been easily addressed by a veteran. For other worries, simple encouragement would have helped keep her spirits up. Box 4.3 lists ways to improve one's coping skills.

BOX 4.3

Ways for a Teacher to Improve Coping

1. Improve time-management techniques

2. Learn from colleagues

3. Adapt relaxation and stress-management strategies

4. Continue professional development to become a more proficient teacher

---

Improving Time Management

Despite insistence that there is no time for planning, a new teacher must be encouraged to *find* that time. Without putting both in-school and out-of-school activities on a schedule, priorities may not be achieved, and teachers will continue to feel worn out, unable to accomplish all of their goals in a day. They should identify activities, both personal and job related, to achieve their goals. The mentor can help the beginning teacher set priorities, estimate the time required for those activities, and establish a realistic schedule. Spending a few minutes at the end of the day to prepare a to-do list for the next day is well worth the time.

In contrast to Miss Jacobs, some teachers find themselves stressed when they do not get the work done because they have *too much* of a social life. They come late to school and leave early, never take anything home, and let their students correct all of their own work. A mentor needs to step in when this happens as well, again assisting the beginner in better time management.

Learning From Colleagues

A mentor can share all kinds of ideas with a beginning teacher—or put the mentee in touch with another teacher who has worked on a similar project. Even if Mr. Bennett did not help Miss Jacobs, perhaps another third-grade teacher could have—or a teacher from another grade level may have had experience planning a similar project. A mentor could direct the beginning teacher to teachers who would be receptive to questions or might have made Mr. Bennett aware of Miss Jacobs's unapparent stress. Finally, a mentor with a history at a given site may well know which teachers have taught which grade levels in the past, regardless of their current level.

Improving Relaxation and Stress-Management Strategies

If stress is related to something that the teacher can control, defining the cause can be the beginning of alleviating the problem. A teacher who is stressed by piled-up paperwork, for example, may need to make a priority of dealing with paper as it comes in. If the teacher does not know *how* to deal with the forms, a mentor aware of the problem can give assistance. If the stress is related to daily routine, a change might help: An art project in the middle of the day, for example, could break up the schedule. Even a change to the physical appearance of a room may improve the teacher's feelings.

If the source of stress is not controllable—for example, if pending conferences are the cause—other techniques might work. Some teachers use meditation or other relaxation methods, stretching, deep breathing, deep muscle massage, exercise, or a healthful diet. Whatever the choice, beginning teachers must take time away from the job for themselves; they must find a balance between their professional and personal lives. A treat of a movie, a sporting event, a concert, or a night out for dinner might do the trick. Some teachers purchase season tickets to a favorite event before the school year begins so they will be sure to set aside time. A mentor can encourage beginning teachers to keep personal activities a priority, as important to their teaching careers as the school routine itself.

CONCLUSION

Every teacher, whether a first-year novice or a veteran of many years, must draw on a wide variety of skills to be effective. Both teaching skills and interpersonal skills are necessary for the teacher to maximize learning time for students and minimize time wasted on classroom management and discipline.

A teacher like Miss Jacobs, who uses her teaching skills to develop a strong lesson plan and her interpersonal skills to get the help she needs, may someday be outstanding in her profession—if she can keep from burning out. To keep her and other beginning teachers on track, a third set of skills—coping skills—is also required. A good mentor can help in all of these areas by providing assistance, answering questions, and offering support and encouragement.

Chapter 5 gives more background regarding context for teacher-mentors—how they fit into broader induction programs. It then discusses strategies to help the new teacher move toward professionalism and suggests variations of mentoring that can be used.

Relax! Only your family expects you to be perfect.

—Advice from a teacher-mentor

5

Moving Toward Professionalism

Our research suggests that the key to addressing [teacher] shortages lies not in active recruitment policies but in support and training for new teachers at the school site. For it is in schools and classrooms where teachers must find success and satisfaction. It is there they will decide whether or not to continue to teach.

—Johnson, Birkeland, Kardos, Kauffman, & Peske (2001, p. 8)

TEACHER INDUCTION PROGRAMS

Mentors throughout the country are increasingly part of induction programs designed to help new teachers get off to a good start in this difficult but rewarding profession. These mentors are one of many components in a comprehensive program designed to help teachers make the transition from preservice education to career. Virtually unheard of two decades ago, induction programs are now responsible not only for keeping teachers on the job but also for helping them develop as professionals. New teachers in a successful induction program will gain the confidence and understanding to want to continue in the field and the skills to work effectively with their students. Box 5.1 lists five common goals for successful induction programs.

Box 5.1

Teacher Induction Program Goals

Five commonly accepted goals of teacher induction programs, as identified by Huling-Austin (1988), are these:

1. To improve teaching performance

2. To increase retention of promising beginning teachers

3. To promote the personal and professional well-being of beginning teachers

4. To transmit the culture of the system to beginning teachers

5. To satisfy mandated requirements related to induction and certifications

---

Ultimately, the goal of any teacher is to help students succeed. With a growing body of research indicating a direct link between student achievement and the quality of a teacher's instruction, the challenge is to "induct large numbers of new colleagues in ways that promote high levels of classroom practice, seek to ensure the academic success of all students, and encourage new ways of being in schools for novice and veteran teachers alike" (Moir & Gless, n.d., p. 1). Teacher induction needs to begin as early as possible in the teacher's career, with professional development continuing throughout the career. Effective programs lead to accomplished professional growth and skilled teachers. In Figure 5.1, a chart from the California Commission on Teacher Credentialing illustrates the role of induction programs in teacher development.

The New Teacher Center of the University of California at Santa Cruz lists on its Web site several components of a quality induction program (Moir & Gless, n.d., pp. 1–5):

- Program vision
- Institutional commitment and support
- Quality mentoring
- Professional standards
- Classroom-based teacher learning

Moir and Gless discuss these components in detail.

Program Vision. Developers of induction programs need to seek not just to retain teachers but to promote "the highest quality of instruction possible." Such programs must not only address teacher survival but also help teachers develop their potential within the educational system.

Figure 5.1   California's learning-to-teach system

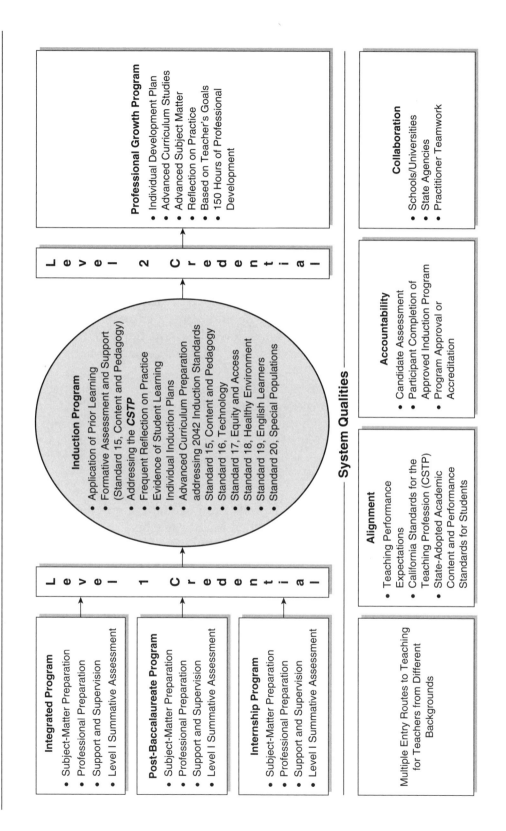

SOURCE: California Commission on Teacher Credentialing.

Institutional Commitment and Support. Teacher learning must be a high priority, with teacher development considered essential, and there must be adequate time and resources to facilitate teacher growth. Administrators of a strong program also avoid the long-time practice of handing new teachers the leftovers after more seasoned teachers have gotten what they want—of giving inappropriate work assignments and conditions to beginners.

Quality Mentoring. Mentors are the most important feature of a high-quality induction program. These experienced leaders must be carefully selected and trained and then must receive ongoing support. They must also have opportunities to develop their own knowledge and skills and to problem-solve.

Professional Standards. Induction programs should adhere to professional standards of practice, such as the California Standards for the Teaching Profession. (See "California State Framework of Teaching Competencies" later in this chapter.) These standards should be used to guide the learning and growth of the teacher. At the same time, local induction programs must keep in mind the complexities and unique needs of the students at their site.

Classroom-Based Teacher Learning. Induction programs are most effective when they can take into consideration the individual needs of a beginning teacher. To help with this, the mentor must know the specific community, school site, and classroom. New teachers learn best while on the job, focusing on their individual work with their particular students in their classroom setting.

When an induction system is well designed and implemented, its effects reach far beyond the new teacher. Mentor-teachers, too, are able to broaden their perspective through observation of new teachers, to articulate the expertise developed through a career, and to reflect on their own work. The program serves, then, to improve the teaching profession overall and sometimes to initiate change in the school culture.

A MODEL: THE SANTA CRUZ NEW TEACHER PROJECT

The Santa Cruz New Teacher Project (SCNTP), begun in 1988, has been praised as a particularly successful teacher induction program. Through this BTSA-affiliated program, some 1,500 K–12 teachers have found support. Led by the Teacher Education Program at the University of California at Santa Cruz, in collaboration with the Santa Cruz County Office of Education, the program serves 16 districts in the Santa Cruz area and the greater Silicon Valley of California. The state provides $3,000 in funds for each beginning teacher in the program, and local school districts contribute an additional $2,100 per new teacher.

According to Janet Gless, associate director of the New Teacher Center at the University of California at Santa Cruz (UCSC), and Ellen Moir, director of Teacher Education at UCSC,

> The quality of the teacher is the single most important ingredient in improving student achievement. An investment in teacher quality needs to start at the earliest stages of a teacher's career and continue throughout a professional lifetime. The work is not just about beginning teachers and induction programs. As our nation hires more than two million new teachers this next decade, we have the chance to transform the teaching profession by creating induction programs that nurture new teachers while promoting the highest standards of classroom teaching (Gless & Moir, n.d., p. 1).

One important aspect of the Santa Cruz New Teacher Project is that veteran teachers are released from all other teaching responsibilities for two to three years while they work with new teachers. Each teacher-mentor is matched with 14 first- and second-year teachers based on grade level and subject matter expertise. These advisers meet with each of the new teachers in their group for about two hours weekly—before, during, or after school. They perform many of the same functions as other teacher-mentors but without needing to find time to do the many responsibilities typically required of teachers. They have time reserved not only to meet with new teachers but also to plan, gather resources, provide other types of support for the new teacher, and communicate with principals.

New teachers in the Santa Cruz program are also given time to observe other teachers, plan curriculum, reflect, self-assess, and attend monthly seminars. These teachers develop a portfolio with the help of their advisers.

The New Teacher Formative Assessment System

At the center of the New Teacher Project induction program is a new teacher professional development system called the New Teacher Center Formative Assessment System (NTC FAS), based on the NTC Developmental Continuum of Teacher Abilities. Mentors use the tools in this system—classroom profiles, collaborative logs, individual learning plans, self-assessment summaries, protocols for collection and analysis of student work, and pre- and postobservation tools—to help beginning teachers.

One-sixth of California BTSA programs use NTC FAS, and it is also used by school districts outside California. Before the opening of school, new mentors receive intensive training focused on using the NTC FAS. They learn to use protocols to observe new teachers, collect student data, and analyze student work to help new teachers plan standards-based instruction. Advanced training in effective coaching skills accompanies this guidance. During the academic year, mentors attend weekly half-day mentor forums, the cornerstone for building mentor skills and abilities. Forums provide additional professional development in such topics as literacy, mentoring for equity, and content-based mentoring. Mentors use this venue to network, share successes and dilemmas, support each other's practice, and ensure that the NTC model continues to evolve to meet current classroom needs. They improve their own practice through the same process of data collection, self-assessment, and revision of practice that they present to new teachers.

Measures of Success

Studies through the years indicate that beginning teachers in the Santa Cruz program have increased job satisfaction, are retained at higher rates, work more effectively with diverse students, and problem-solve better regarding issues of instruction and student achievement. When surveyed, principals indicated that performance of those beginning teachers who go through the program improves significantly. These teachers have higher morale, are more willing to take risks, have better problem-solving skills, have better classroom management and organization, and have more effective instructional strategies than teachers without the benefit of such an induction program. In the SCNTP program, data indicate that the increased effectiveness of beginning teachers, combined with decreased teacher attrition, led after five years to a return on investment of $1.37 per $1 in current dollars (Alliance for Excellent Education, 2004).

Veteran teachers benefit as well, returning to their teaching assignments with renewed passion for teaching, a broader perspective on education, and increased communication and leadership skills. One veteran reported,

> In working with [my colleagues] in a reflective manner, I am becoming more reflective about my own practice and its effects on students. And through our work to implement various strategies, my own repertoire of teaching methods is ever-increasing. When I return to a classroom of students, I will bring with me an enriched and stronger practice.

All of this seems to be adding up to higher success for students. According to a recent study, students of new teachers supported by the SCNTP in one district serving 19,000 students made learning gains similar to the gains of students of more experienced teachers. This was true even though new teachers were more likely to be teaching English Language Learners (Alliance for Excellent Education, 2004).

Keys to Success

Gless and Moir attribute the success of their program to the following:

- The importance of the veteran teacher as adviser
- The full-time role of the veteran
- The link to site administration
- The impact of standards imbedded in a compassionate, supportive environment

They note that the following qualities are essential in their veteran teachers:

- Strong interpersonal skills
- Credibility with peers and administrators
- Demonstrated curiosity and eagerness to learn
- Respect for multiple perspectives
- Outstanding instructional practice

Other essential qualities—observing and coaching skills, knowledge of professional standards, familiarity with the portfolio process, support strategies for new teachers, group facilitation and presentation skills—can be learned later, say Moir and Gless. Full-time release allows these mentors to focus fully on helping new teachers, and commitment and support from site administrators are crucial.

The National Council of States in Education has recognized the SCNTP for excellence, and the California Council on the Education of Teachers has recognized it for its contribution to excellence in education. Because of its success, the Santa Cruz program now serves as a model for new programs being developed in other states, including New York.

FROM NOVICE TO PROFESSIONAL

Beginning teachers do not assume their first teaching assignments as autonomous professionals. And even some veteran teachers experience situations in which their resourcefulness is at a low ebb. Professional growth . . . occurs developmentally and individually over time. Growth is supported through mediated experiences by skilled leaders in workshops, course work, reading, study, and collaboration and modeling in the school environment (Costa & Garmston, 1994, p. 165).

Although the new teacher's first year is often spent trying just to survive, the goal of an induction program is really to build professionalism.

Ultimately, a good induction program should not only provide new teachers with support but also help them develop professional skills through a highly individualized approach. Mentors should ask themselves frequently, "What more could this teacher do to help students learn better—and how could I make that process easier?"

According to the California Department of Education, "Experienced teachers need high-quality, research-based, sustained professional growth to remain effective teachers" (2006, p. 9). In a white paper on developing highly qualified teachers and administrators for California schools, the department notes that the most promising means of professional growth for both new and experienced teachers are through coaching (or mentors) and professional learning communities. Mentors have an opportunity to provide content-focused professional development.

In many districts, new teachers are required to participate in several structured days of induction during the summer, focused on the first days of school. Seminars may deal with classroom management, planning and effective teaching, and local policies and procedures. Follow-up professional development sessions are typically provided in the district during the new teacher's first two or three years.

In many states, new teachers also participate in state-sponsored training activities, such as content-specific beginning teacher seminars, online professional development resources, and portfolio assessment conferences. Professional development seminars allow beginning teachers to deepen their understanding of state standards and portfolio requirements through structured collaborations with peers and seminar leaders.

In addition, under the Reading First initiative of No Child Left Behind, many districts provide district-based workshops regarding the teaching of literacy. Many districts feel that new teachers have inadequate preservice preparation in literacy strategies, especially secondary teachers who are not typically well trained to teach literacy across the curriculum.

Although mentors often provide emotional support and help with classroom management, their goal should always be the ongoing professional development of the mentee—to focus the beginning teacher on improving instruction. Even for first-year teachers, mentors can concentrate on lesson planning, analyzing student work, collecting and analyzing classroom data, and revising instruction. They can also co-teach, provide demonstration lessons, arrange for observation of exemplary teachers, facilitate relationships with principals, and provide access to district and community resources. For second-year teachers, mentor support can place greater emphasis on content-specific pedagogy and differentiating instruction.

Some of the standards, federal and statewide, that have been set for professional teachers are described below. These are goals that all should strive toward, and a good mentor can help the new teacher reach them.

The Interstate New Teacher
Assessment and Support Consortium

In the mid-1990s, professional educators from all 50 states joined together as a group called the Interstate New Teacher Assessment and Support Consortium (INTASC). The group developed the following 10 standards for what every teacher should know and be able to do:

1. The teacher understands the central concepts, tools of inquiry, and structures of the discipline(s) he or she teaches and can create learning experiences that make these aspects of subject matter meaningful for students.

2. The teacher understands how children learn and develop, and can provide learning opportunities that support their intellectual, social, and personal development.

3. The teacher understands how students differ in their approaches to learning and creates instructional opportunities that are adapted to diverse learners.

4. The teacher understands and uses a variety of instructional strategies to encourage students' development of critical thinking, problem-solving, and performance skills.

5. The teacher uses an understanding of individual and group motivation and behavior to create a learning environment that encourages positive social interaction, active engagement in learning, and self-motivation.

6. The teacher uses knowledge of effective verbal, nonverbal, and media communication techniques to foster active inquiry, collaboration, and supportive interaction in the classroom.

7. The teacher plans instruction based on knowledge of subject matter, students, the community, and curriculum goals.

8. The teacher understands and uses formal and informal assessment strategies to evaluate and ensure the continuous intellectual, social, and physical development of the learner.

9. The teacher is a reflective practitioner who continually evaluates the effects of his or her choices and actions on others (students, parents, and other professionals in the learning community) and who actively seeks out opportunities to grow professionally.

10. The teacher fosters relationships with school colleagues, parents, and agencies in the larger community to support students' learning and well-being.

Since the publication of these standards, many states have used them as the basis for their certification and professional development of new teachers. "This effort took another step toward creating a coherent approach to educating and licensing teachers based upon shared views among the states and within the profession of what constitutes professional teaching" (INTASC, 1992).

California State Framework of Teaching Competencies

The following framework, developed originally in 1992, outlines the knowledge, skills, and abilities expected of effective teachers in California. Similar to frameworks used in most states, it is based on a four-year pilot project of the Far West Laboratory for Educational Research and Development (now WestEd, the federal Region XI Comprehensive Assistance Center serving Northern California) for the California Beginning Teacher Support and Assessment (BTSA) program. The framework is intended to (1) enhance the success of new teachers in California by defining a vision of effective beginning teaching and (2) provide a common language and a new vision of the scope and complexity of teaching in order to facilitate the induction of beginning teachers into their professional roles and responsibilities. The framework specifies six related dimensions or domains. Together these six standards represent a developmental, holistic view of teaching. They are designed to be used by teachers to

- prompt reflection about student learning and teaching practice;
- formulate professional goals to improve teaching practice; and
- guide, monitor, and assess the progress of a teacher's practice toward professional goals and professionally accepted benchmarks.

In July 1997, the State Board of Education adopted this original BTSA framework as the new California Standards for the Teaching Profession. The six interrelated categories of teaching competence are as follows:

1. *Engaging and Supporting All Students in Powerful Learning.* The teacher builds on knowledge of students, subject matter, teaching, and learning to enact effective and powerful learning opportunities with all students. Varied teaching strategies and approaches are used to encourage all students to demonstrate what has been learned in meaningful and authentic ways.

2. *Creating and Maintaining an Effective Environment for Student Learning.* The teacher creates and maintains a smoothly functioning, safe learning environment in which students assume responsibility for themselves and one another, participate in decision making, work collaboratively and independently, are treated fairly and respectfully, and engage in purposeful learning activities. Student expectations for behavior are clearly

established, understood, and consistently maintained. The physical environment and the arrangements within that environment support positive social interactions and facilitate equitable engagement of students in productive tasks.

3. *Understanding and Organizing Subject Matter Knowledge for Student Learning.* The teacher exhibits strong working knowledge of subject matter content to be taught and is able to use that knowledge to construct meaningful learning activities, products, and long-term projects for all students. Students understand the central themes and concepts within a content area and are able to apply those learnings to other content areas in authentic ways.

4. *Planning Instruction and Designing Learning Experiences for All Students.* The teacher plans instruction based on knowledge of subject matter, students, and community. The richness of student diversity is reflected in the planning process. Challenging but realistic goals are established for all students, and instructional plans are designed to help students reach those goals.

5. *Assessing Student Learning.* The teacher establishes and clearly communicates performance expectations and collects information about student performance from a variety of sources. The teacher shares that information with students, parents, and support personnel in ways that improve understanding and foster continued growth and development. The teacher adjusts instruction based on assessment information to ensure enhanced learning opportunities for students.

6. *Developing as a Professional Educator.* The teacher reflects on his or her own professional development as he or she interacts in a wider learning environment with students, other educators, parents, and community members. The teacher recognizes his or her responsibility to the broader professional community and seeks to learn from and contribute to that community and to improve teaching and learning for all students.

Interested new teachers and mentors should contact the California Department of Education to obtain the complete, updated *California Standards for the Teaching Profession* (or contact the department of education for other states as appropriate). In the *California Standards*, each competency dimension is introduced in a narrative description of best practice that portrays an accomplished level of professional teaching. Following the narrative description, each standard is organized in elements that identify key areas within that domain of teaching. Each element is further specified with questions that encourage teachers to explore aspects of teaching practice throughout their careers. To foster ongoing reflection and insights into teaching, the questions are introduced with the stem "How do I . . . ?" The questions can also be phrased as "Why do I . . . ?," which encourages teachers to examine the rationale for key aspects of their teaching.

Federal Policy: No Child Left Behind

Virtually every teacher entering the profession since 2002 has been touched by the requirements of the federal No Child Left Behind (NCLB) law enacted in October 2002. Under this law, every state and school district must be committed to providing a "highly qualified teacher" for every student in a core-content classroom. To ensure that teachers are qualified, schools are implementing rigorous, standards-aligned teacher preparation and induction, as well as mentoring for teachers and administrators; professional development to enhance and maintain educator effectiveness; and innovative programs to recruit and retain talented, highly qualified teachers. With this mandate came an era of testing and accountability that is likely to endure, most officials believe.

Strategies for Building Professionalism

Integration of professional development should be ongoing, incorporated in staff development programs as well as in more focused work on particular instructional skills. Development must include helping the new teacher increase content knowledge, master instructional techniques, and understand how students learn. Following are just a few of the areas in which a mentor-teacher might help a novice develop professionally:

Setting Goals. To develop professionally, teachers should set specific goals. Heller recommends setting two or three goals in a year—one related to institutional (school-wide) objectives and the other more personal (2004, p. 73). A good mentor can help the new teacher determine specific measurable goals, assist in attaining those goals, and help with documentation. For example, a new teacher might decide to implement a particular writing program in class (institutional goal) and to improve time-management skills (personal goal). A mentor might ask questions to help the teacher define those goals, establish a plan of action, and set criteria for measuring mastery. For more on helping the mentee develop an action plan, see Chapter 8, Practical Strategies for Assisting New Teachers. See also Appendix B, Mentor-Mentee Action Plans.

Locating Resources. Mentors should provide information for mentees about workshops and courses available to help them improve their skills. It is also helpful to share information about professional associations worth joining, as well as useful journals, magazines, books, and videos, particularly those relevant to the grade level or subject matter. Many of these resources can help the beginning teacher improve efficiency and gain confidence. In some programs, mentors have available to them funds to use to help mentees with professional development. At times it can be especially meaningful for the mentor and mentee to participate together in workshops or conferences or in visitations to demonstration projects. Mentors provide a great service when they share information about available resources.

Engaging in Discussion/Reflection. On a regular basis, the mentor and new teacher should meet to discuss professional goals, share ideas and strategies on effective practice, reflect on current methods, share on-the-job observations, and discuss tactics for improvement. These discussions are most helpful when mentor and mentee set goals and procedures together based on the mentee's individual ideas about professional development (Guskey, 2000, p. 28).

It is optimal if the mentoring program provides common planning and collaboration time for mentor-mentee teams. During this time, new teachers can work with the mentor as well as with other colleagues to examine multiple sources of data about teaching, including lesson plans, student work, use of assessments, and teacher reflection about teaching and learning.

Developing Portfolios. Teachers wanting to demonstrate professional competence may need to develop a portfolio of work and related materials. Evidence of teacher proficiency may come in the form of journal entries, student feedback surveys, documented observations, lesson plans, pictures, video- and audiotapes, a professional project, an annotated bibliography, photographs, copies of overheads and other presentation materials, and/or student work. An experienced teacher can help newer teachers develop, collect, and select samples to demonstrate professional achievement. In addition to demonstrating competence, the process of developing the portfolio can help the teacher in self-assessment. "The science portfolio forced me to do something that is not instinctive for me at this point in my teaching career," one beginning teacher commented. "The portfolio forced me to immediately reflect on how the day's lesson was perceived by my students. Furthermore, the portfolio allowed me to identify certain strengths and weaknesses in my teaching" (Alliance for Excellent Education, 2004).

MENTORING PROGRAMS FOR PROFESSIONAL GROWTH

Like teachers new to the profession, teachers who have moved beyond the novice stage may benefit from working with a mentor. Teachers exhibiting weaknesses may work with a mentor to overcome shortcomings, for example, and to work toward professional goals. Seasoned teachers who simply want to develop professionally may also benefit from working with other teachers to enhance their skills. Following are suggestions for professional growth among seasoned teachers. These are only a few of the possibilities.

Learning Groups

In a variation of support groups, seasoned teachers may meet in groups to work on professional development, such as literacy. According to the

International Reading Association (2003, p. 1), "Teachers want to engage in activities that develop and foster professionalism, that provide opportunities for them to study their own learning, that permit them to collaborate with colleagues, and that focus on more effective instruction to serve all students." The International Reading Association provides resources for educators in the areas of literacy and advocates study groups as a way for teachers to pursue deeper understanding of literacy topics. In this approach, teachers receive resources to read, write about what they learn, share with other teachers having similar interests, and then share with students.

Co-Mentoring

This variation, also called *peer coaching,* brings together two or more veteran teachers with the "sole purpose" to "mutually enhance teaching and learning effectiveness—veteran teachers can break the isolation of the classroom and look at their practices through safe, objective and friendly eyes" (Portner, 2001, p. 95). This variation is nonhierarchical; that is, individual participants give and take from roughly the same level of experience.

Critical Friends

The Annenberg Institute for School Reform at Brown University developed the idea of critical friends groups. These groups bring together some five to eight teachers and a facilitator (internal or external). The teachers meet to examine samples of student work or instructional programs and concerns over the course of a school year or longer. The teachers become familiar with each other's classrooms and serve as peer coaches (Glickman, 2002, p. 17).

Peer Assistance and Review (PAR)

PAR coaches not only mentor but also evaluate teachers. They work with both new and veteran teachers who need to improve their knowledge and skills. In these programs, consulting teachers support mentees through observing, modeling, sharing ideas and skills, and recommending materials for further study. One significant difference between PAR coaches and mentors, however, is that "consulting teachers conduct formal evaluations and make recommendations regarding the continued employment of participating teachers" (Portner 2001, p. 96). The PAR coach, then, is more like a supervisor than a mentor and often does not share the vital components of trust and confidentiality so important in mentoring.

CONCLUSION

New teacher-mentors are often one component of a larger teacher induction program, recognized as essential to retaining teachers and helping them develop into skilled professionals. It is important for mentors to see how they fit into this larger context and to understand the significance of their work. It is also important to see how these programs can continue to assist the teacher in developing professionally even after those first apprehensive years. This chapter also introduces some variations on mentor-mentee relationships that benefit seasoned professionals wanting to advance their career skills.

This chapter concludes Part I, which addresses the need for good mentors and how mentors fit into the broader scope of teacher induction and development. Part II gives practical advice for mentors to use in working with new teachers: Working as a Partner With the Adult Learner (Chapter 6), Stages in Teacher Development (Chapter 7), Practical Strategies for Assisting New Teachers (Chapter 8), and Overcoming Obstacles and Reaping the Rewards (Chapter 9).

PART II

Effective Strategies for the Good Mentor

6

Working as a Partner With the Adult Learner

Teaching was the fulfillment of a lifelong dream for Sherie, 40, a first-year elementary school teacher. When Sherie was an intern, her site principal noticed her strong teaching abilities, outgoing personality, and unusual dedication. He took a personal interest in her teaching career, offered her advice during her internship, and encouraged her to stay at his school site during her first official year of teaching.

As the teacher of a first- and second-grade combination class with students from many language backgrounds, Sherie worked diligently at maintaining each learner's ethnic integrity. In Saturday seminars, she participated in learning activities based on the *California Standards for the Teaching Profession* (California Commission on Teacher Credentialing and the California Department of Education, 1997). Sherie used the standards to assess her own teaching, and she developed a classroom-research questionnaire to foster her professional growth: "How can I develop teaching strategies that address different student learning styles?" Over the year, she compiled student work and evidence of her teaching practices into a teaching portfolio (WestEd, 1997).

During her first year of teaching, Sherie had two mentors: her principal and her mentor in the Beginning Educators' Seminars on Teaching (BEST) program. Each held regular conversations with her, observed her teaching, listened to her concerns, and offered advice when she asked for it. They provided different perspectives, two backdrops from which she could view teaching as her chosen profession. Latisha, her BEST mentor, conducted four formal, standards-based observations of Sherie's teaching as it related to her research questions. She offered Sherie emotional support and suggestions for classroom management, curriculum planning, assessment, and educational materials. Latisha helped Sherie understand how to meet state and district curriculum standards while individualizing instruction of her culturally diverse students. She reinforced the BEST seminars' emphasis on the importance of reflective conversations and writing. Sherie completed her first year of teaching with a deeper understanding of school and a greater trust in administration than are usually present in novice teachers.

—Scherer (1999, pp. 116–117)

A good teacher of children is not necessarily a good mentor of another teacher. Needed above and beyond expertise in teaching is the ability to facilitate the learning of adults. Good mentors stray from the traditional "authoritarian teacher/supplicant learner" archetype. They work on establishing a collaborative learning partnership with their mentee, grounded in knowledge about adult learning.

Adult learning, or *andragogy,* is rooted in principles delineated by Malcolm Knowles (1980) in *The Modern Practice of Adult Education: From Pedagogy to Andragogy.* Knowles points out that adult learners bring their own history of experience to a learning relationship. They learn best when they are engaged as active partners, not when they serve as passive receivers. A good mentor seldom acts as an authority figure, but more often serves as a facilitator, a "guide on the side," rather than a "sage" on or off a stage. Adult mentees—even those initially unsure of themselves and needing extensive support—require as adults as much self-direction as possible, with involvement in diagnosing, planning, implementing, and evaluating their own learning. Portner notes that they also tend to be goal oriented, constantly looking for relevance in learning (2006, p. 14), and that many adults struggle with self-esteem issues and bring with them memories of bad experiences in traditional education as well as a preoccupation with events outside the classroom (p. 15).

Effective mentors of adult learners understand that their role is mainly one of facilitation. In a dynamic facilitative process, a mentor-mentee learning partnership evolves over time as the developing teacher becomes more and more comfortable and self-directed. Facilitation involves

- encouraging beginning teachers to set their own learning objectives,
- involving beginning teachers in planning how they will learn,
- encouraging beginning teachers to use a wide variety of resources to get to their objectives, and
- helping beginning teachers implement and evaluate their learning.

Beginning teachers want to be treated as equals to their colleagues, and it is extremely important when mentoring to treat the mentee as a partner, an equal in the learning process. "The legitimate recognition that [beginning teachers] should be actively involved as both planners and participants in their own learning continues to have a deservedly important impact on the theory and practice of adult education and, by extension, of adult mentoring," writes Cohen (1995, p. 10). A mentee will not necessarily grow in ability or in desire to improve simply because a mentor has discussed a topic or a goal. Rather, the mentor and mentee need to work through ideas together, both fully participating in the process. Experienced mentors report a "balancing act," in which they carefully adjust their mentoring behaviors so as not to tilt the relationship into either inappropriate control or an unrealistic "hands-off" position. Adult learning requires time for trial and error, reflection, and self-correction. Effective mentors respect their mentees' singular learning curves. They watch for appropriate timing, keeping in mind that the new, often overwhelmed teacher must be ready to grow from the process before any "teaching" can occur. The mentor, in other words, must present suggestions at a time when the mentee is ready to absorb them.

BELIEFS ABOUT SUPERVISION AND MENTORING

Methods of supervising teachers are changing radically from those used in the 1980s, when school administrators observed teachers in their classrooms to see how they were doing. "The pattern of the 1980s—when principals were encouraged to be 'instructional leaders' and teacher evaluation and staff development programs were built on 'effective teaching' research—is being challenged," writes John O'Neil (1993, p. 1). "So is the appropriateness of principals' serving dual roles, supervising teachers in the administrative sense (evaluating their performance, for example) while also trying to help them improve their instruction." As a result, experts say, traditional forms of supervision are being questioned. New avenues to teacher growth are more peer oriented and less likely to fit comfortably under the mantle of supervision.

Whereas supervision in the 1980s was based on the evaluation model, most mentoring today is based more closely on some combination of clinical supervision and cognitive coaching models. A quick summary of these models reveals some of their important differences and provides a background for further discussion.

The Evaluation Model. In the traditional evaluation model, the board of trustees and the state or province initiate an evaluation, and only personnel holding an administrative credential are authorized to evaluate. Districts set up policies and deadlines for evaluation of teachers as a way of meeting contractual requirements and controlling quality. Commonly, an evaluator rates the teacher based on standards developed, negotiated, adopted, and made public. Performance behaviors to be evaluated might include punctuality, willingness to participate in extracurricular and professional activities, personal characteristics, professional attitudes and growth, and so on. The evaluator observes the teacher based on the criteria established by the district and enters ratings on a preprinted form. Copies of the evaluation go to the teacher, to the teacher's personnel file, and to the building principal. Teachers receive ratings such as outstanding, adequate, or needs to improve (Costa & Garmston, 1994, p. 14).

Clinical Supervision. Under this model, an administrator or another supervisor trained in the techniques of clinical supervision works with the teacher to determine objectives, concepts, techniques, materials, and assessment methods. The supervisor then observes in-class instruction, analyzes the data to determine patterns of behavior and critical incidents of teaching and learning, and confers with the new teacher to share the data. The cycle continues, with more planning to determine future directions for growth (Glatthorn, 1984, pp. 7–8). Clinical supervision "is an intensive process designed to improve instruction by conferring with the teacher on lesson planning, observing the lesson, analyzing the observational data, and giving the teacher feedback about the observation" (Glatthorn, 1984, p. 7).

Cognitive Coaching. In the cognitive coaching model, new teachers allow themselves to be coached by someone who is respected for being helpful and having good leadership qualities. The coach may be a department chair or a peer. Coaching begins on the new teacher's first day on the job and can continue throughout the year. Under this model, new teachers determine criteria relating to student and teacher behavior for the coach to observe. Such behaviors might include classroom interaction, instruction, student learning, student performance, curriculum adherence, individual student behavior, teacher behavior and skills, and so on. New teachers let the mentor-coach know what they would like the coach to look for and what feedback would be helpful. After observation, the coach shares any information collected with the new teachers, who self-evaluate based on the criteria established in a planning period. The goal is to improve instruction, curriculum, and student learning (Costa & Garmston, 1994, p. 14).

Costa and Garmston (1994) outline the following steps in the cognitive coaching cycle:

1. The planning conference (Costa & Garmston, 1994, pp. 18–20): The initial conference is a period for building trust. During this conference, coaches focus attention on new teachers' goals. As the new teachers discuss their lessons, they refine their strategies, discover potential problems, and essentially "rehearse" (mentally work through) their upcoming lesson.

They also establish the parameters for a reflecting conference to follow the observation and set the agenda for that meeting. The planning conference forces new teachers to think about their instruction plans and promote future self-coaching.

2. Observation of the lesson (Costa & Garmston, 1994, p. 21): During this step, the coach collects data as requested by the teacher and discussed in the planning conference. The idea is for the new teachers to experiment with their own strategies and techniques, with the coach gathering data.

3. The reflecting conference (Costa & Garmston, 1994, pp. 21–22): This follow-up conference, according to Costa and Garmston, is best if delayed somewhat after the observation to allow time for the teacher to reflect and analyze and for the coach to organize data and plan the reflective coaching strategy. To begin this conference, the new teachers share their impressions of the lesson and specific examples supporting those impressions. They are asked to compare what occurred during the lesson with what was planned. Ideally, the coach helps beginning teachers draw conclusions regarding relationships between their actions and student outcomes. Finally, the new teachers are encouraged to project how new insights will affect future lessons and also to reflect on the coaching process itself.

The Mentor. The traditional mentoring role, then, is based on the model of clinical supervision, with mentoring strategies often following the model of cognitive coaching. The mentee takes an active role, suggesting topics to be addressed; the mentor observes and collects data; and the two meet to reflect, learn, and grow. This formal process can greatly enhance a teacher's ability to apply what is learned to the classroom. According to researchers Joyce and Showers (Albert, Blondino, & McGrath, 1990), in fact, beginning teachers are most likely to use what they know if coaching is built into the staff development process (see Table 6.1).

Table 6.1   Effectiveness of Training Components

	Knowledge	Workshop Application	Classroom Use
Theory	100%	5%	5%
Theory plus demonstration	100%	5%	5%
Theory, demonstration, and practice with feedback	100%	85–90%	5–10%
Theory, demonstration, and practice with feedback and coaching	100%	85–90%	75–85%

SOURCE: From the research of Joyce & Showers, as cited in Albert, Blondino, & McGrath (1990).

In Appendix C, The Supervisory Beliefs Inventory, Glickman (1985) presents a self-assessment for supervisors interested in discovering their own orientation in supervision. Although Glickman uses the term "supervision," much of what he says applies to mentoring as well.

PHASES IN THE MENTORING RELATIONSHIP: THREE MODELS

The core of mentoring . . . is the focus on collaborative participation and mutual critical thinking and reflection about the process, value, and results of jointly derived learning goals established for the mentee.

—Norman H. Cohen (1995, p. 14)

Mentors and their mentees go through predictable phases in their relationship as it develops and matures over time. Where they are in these phases will determine strategies to be used by the mentor. Cohen (1995, pp. 15–16) describes the following four phases:

1. The early phase: In the beginning, the mentor-mentee pair focuses primarily on building a trusting relationship. Mentees must feel comfortable with their mentor and trust that they will not be judged when they seek help.

2. The middle phase: Once the mentee is comfortable, the partners exchange information. The mentor accumulates knowledge about the mentee in an effort to understand the mentee's goals and concerns.

3. The later phase: The mentor explores the interests and beliefs of the mentee and attempts to learn the reasons for the mentee's decisions. This might include inviting the mentee to self-appraise.

4. The last phase: The mentor motivates mentees to reflect on their goals, to pursue challenges, and to follow through on their own personal, educational, and career path.

How quickly a mentee is ready to move from one of these phases to the next varies considerably, depending on the individual. A perceptive mentor will be aware of the mentee's readiness to move on and will let that readiness guide the progression of the relationship.

The Association for Supervision and Curriculum Development (ASCD, 1999a) presents a different model of mentee learning, also breaking the mentor-mentee relationship into four phases. Like Cohen, ASCD's (1999a) *Mentoring to Improve Schools* emphasizes the need for the mentor to be aware of the mentee's progression and to time interventions accordingly. "Be a good listener and ask questions to continually assess the developmental needs of the protégé, the state of mentoring, and the most appropriate mentoring response," ASCD advises.

The four phases of this model (ASCD, 1999a, pp. 103, 105) are as follows:

1. In the beginning, mentors and mentees start to develop their relationship, with the mentors taking primary responsibility for leadership. The new teachers are just beginning their careers and may well move quickly from excited anticipation of their job into a period of stress and survival. They are most likely to ask basic questions with only one correct answer (e.g., "How do I let the office know how many kids are absent?"). In this phase, mentors provide information as needed and model for the mentees and then move on to help the mentees set priorities and direction (e.g., how to conduct a class meeting, prepare for a parent conference, or set up a grade book).

2. Later, mentees and mentors build a partnership. Often new teachers by this time are disillusioned with their jobs and question the way things are (e.g., "Help! Got any ideas for dealing with this unruly student behavior?"). Mentors offer assistance (e.g., providing samples of classroom discipline policies), but at the same time seek suggestions from the mentee. They attempt to let the mentee take more responsibility for the relationship.

3. As the mentor-mentee relationship becomes strong, the two enjoy working together, sharing ideas, analyzing, and making decisions together (e.g., "Why do we have so many assemblies? It's hard to get the kids focused back on classwork afterward. I'm losing too much valuable class time!"). The mentor helps with prioritizing but defers to the mentee's judgment whenever possible. The mentee is in a period of rejuvenation.

4. The mentor begins to withdraw from the relationship, encouraging the mentee to become independent. The mentor now uses questions to encourage analysis and reflection from the mentee (e.g., asks the new teacher how a new strategy might affect student learning; listens as the new teacher discusses an assessment of examples of student work; engages the new teacher in a reflective conversation about an issue or concern). The mentor defers to the mentee's judgment and affirms the mentee's abilities and understanding. By this time, the mentee is often headed back into a period of anticipation and is ready for self-growth (see Figure 6.1).

Figure 6.1   Dynamics within the mentoring process

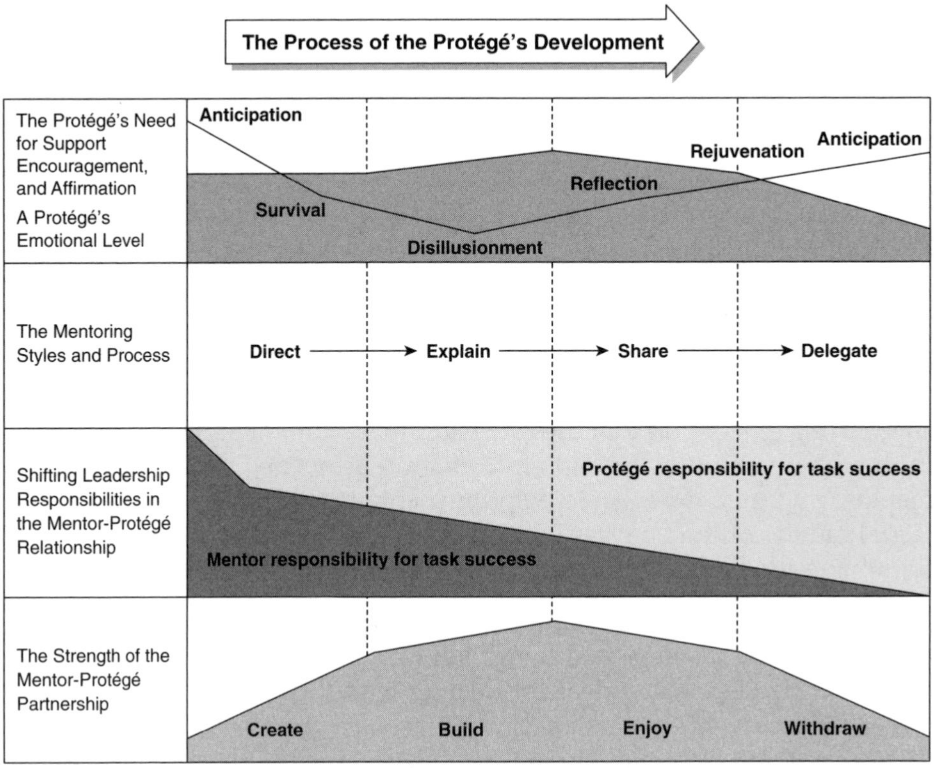

SOURCE: From *Mentoring to Improve Schools: Facilitator's Guide* (p. 105). Alexandria, VA: ASCD, 1999. Used with permission. The Association for Supervision and Curriculum Development is a worldwide community of educators advocating sound policies and sharing best practices to achieve the success of each learner. To learn more, visit ASCD at www.ascd.org.

Joyce and Showers (1982, 1983) and Showers (1985) characterize the process of coaching or mentoring as a similar phased-in approach. They describe five functions:

1. *Providing companionship.* The first function of mentoring is to "provide interchange with another human being over a difficult process" (Joyce & Showers, 1983, p. 19). The mentoring relationship involves mutual reflection, the checking of perceptions, the sharing of frustrations and successes, and the informal thinking through of problems. When one person watches another try a new model of teaching for the first time, for instance, the two will find much to talk about. Companionship provides reassurance that problems are normal. It not only makes the new teacher's learning process technically easier but also enhances the quality of the experience. "It is more pleasurable to share a new thing than to do it in

isolation. The lonely business of teaching has sorely lacked the companionship that we envision for our coaching teams" (Joyce & Showers, 1983, p. 19). Companionship also helps overcome the tendency to avoid the awkwardness of practicing a new strategy.

2. *Giving technical feedback.* In the course of their relationship, the team will reach the stage where the mentor will provide feedback based on observations of the mentee's teaching. This technical feedback is not to be confused with general evaluation. Feedback does not imply judgment about the overall quality of teaching, but is confined to information about the execution of specific skills. The mentor might point out omissions, examine how materials are arranged, check to see whether all parts of a teaching strategy have been brought together, and so on. Technical feedback keeps the mind of the developing teacher on the business of perfecting skills, polishing them, and working through problem areas. Whether the mentee is trying a new model of teaching, implementing a new curriculum, or setting up a classroom management system, feedback must be accurate, specific, and nonjudgmental.

3. *Analyzing application and extending executive control.* As the new teacher's skills develop and solidify, mentoring moves into a more complex stage: mutual examination of the appropriate use of new strategies:

> The cognitive aspects of transferring new behaviors into effective classroom practice are more difficult than the interactive moves of teaching. While all teachers can develop skill in performing a new teaching strategy fairly readily, the harder tasks come as the skill is applied in the classroom (Showers, 1985, p. 14).

One of the important things a new teacher learns is when to use a new model appropriately and what will be achieved by doing so. Selecting the right occasions to use a teaching strategy is not as easy as it sounds. For instance, the new teacher may have learned in college about inductive teaching strategies, such as concept attainment, and may have had little difficulty learning the pattern of the models and discussing the models with materials provided. But it is a different task for beginning teachers to select concepts to teach in their own classrooms, reorganize materials from the standard textbook, teach students to respond to the new strategy, and create lessons they have never seen demonstrated directly. In this phase, these tasks become the substance of conversations between the new and the experienced teachers. The new teacher is developing what Joyce and Showers (1982, 1983) call executive control—that is, a "meta understanding" about how the strategy works, how it can be fitted into their instructional repertoire, and how to modify or create instructional materials for its use. Executive control comes with the new teacher's growing judgment and competence.

4. *Adapting to the students.* New teachers expend much energy trying to figure out how best to apply new teaching strategies to their particular group of students. Successful teaching means that students are responding successfully. Mentors can help new teachers adapt strategies to fit the needs of their students and can suggest ways of acquainting students with what is expected of them:

> One of the major functions of the coach is to help [the mentee] to "read" the responses of the students to make decisions about skill training and how to adapt the model. This is especially important in the early stages of practice when teachers are concerned with their own behavior and it is difficult to worry about the students as well (Joyce & Showers, 1982, p. 7).

5. *Facilitating.* Successfully implementing any new teaching method requires practice. Mentors should expect that a new teacher's early tries will not come close to reaching standards. With this in mind, Joyce and Showers (1982) point out that a major job of mentors is to help their mentees feel good about themselves during these early trials. "Teachers' lack of interpersonal support and close contact with others in the context of teaching is a tragedy. Coaching reduces this isolation and increases support" (p. 7).

In his book, *Mentor: Guiding the Journey of Adult Learners,* Laurent Daloz (1999) explains facilitation this way:

> It is very important to watch for the growing edge, like a coach photographing their forward movement and replaying it for them. This may mean being very explicit about what [mentees] have done well. It is generally more effective to show people when they are on track than to tell them where they should go or to criticize when they have strayed. Emphasize positive movement, underline it, restate it, praise it. By spending undue time on the negative, we run the risk of helping our [mentees] construct a vision of the impossible, whereas our job is to help them imagine the possible and then move toward it. Always we are guides, encouraging movement (pp. 123–124).

All three of these mentoring models move along a continuum to a more facilitative approach. The goal is autonomy for the beginning teacher to self-assess and self-prescribe. The mentor assumes different support and assessment roles at different stages of the continuum of the relationship. In the early stages, information tends to flow from mentor to the beginning teacher, with the mentor offering suggestions and solutions. As the beginning teacher develops increasing autonomy, the relationship becomes more collaborative, with the beginning teacher and the mentor reflecting and co-constructing solutions. See Chapter 7, Stages in Teacher Development, for more on specific developmental patterns within the profession.

GETTING TO TRUST

Trust: assured reliance on the character, ability, strength, or truth of someone or something.

—*Merriam Webster's Collegiate Dictionary,* 10th ed.

In each of the mentoring sequences just described, the pattern of an evolving relationship is built on a foundation of trust. Feelings of jitteriness, tension, fear, and nervousness have no place in the relationship. Trust is a vital aspect of school life that influences basic patterns of interpersonal and group behavior. From the beginning, mentors need to establish trust between themselves and the new teachers with whom they work. Trust is a fundamental feature of mentoring and pervades all successful mentor-protégé relationships (see Box 6.1). As one San Francisco mentor put it, "You must get to trust, or you get nowhere."

BOX 6.1

Trust

- Trust is built by focusing directly on it.
- Taking risks is necessary to build trust.
- Getting supported for taking risks builds trust.
- Allowing yourself to be vulnerable increases others' trust of you.
- Caring about each other is necessary to establish trust.
- Letting go of negative incidents in the past is critical to trust building.

To establish trust, a mentor must demonstrate openness, honesty, and candor. Such openness breeds confidence and trust: A person who seeks to conceal nothing does not, in all likelihood, seek to harm others. Effective mentors are willing to be treated as human beings and do not tend to hide behind the cloak of bureaucratic power and seniority. Such candor and authenticity promote a climate of trust and intimacy. In a trusting relationship, beginning teachers believe that they can depend on the mentor in difficult situations, that they can rely on the integrity of this new colleague, and that confidentiality will not be broken. In contrast, a mentor displaying inauthentic behavior has been characterized as "playing the role," "manipulating and using people and the system," "passing the buck," and "blaming others for his own mistakes and shortfalls." See Box 6.2 for a list of ways to build trust.

BOX 6.2

A Menu of Trust Builders

- Ensure—and keep—confidentiality.
- Hold regular team meetings, with both task and trust issues on the agenda.
- Clarify expectations.
- Discuss expectations.
- Negotiate expectations.
- Be congruent. Walk the talk.
- Create multidirectional communications.
- Respect, honor, and celebrate each individual's style.
- Confront directly with caring.
- Focus on gains, not losses.
- Describe, don't evaluate.
- Delegate power and authority.
- Admit your own mistakes and vulnerability.
- Be a risk taker when it comes to trusting others.
- Create interactions.
- Share feelings as well as thoughts.
- Accept that we all get frustrated and angry at times.
- Encourage balance and renewal for the team and for each individual.
- Celebrate—even mistakes.
- Practice openness.
- Play, laugh, and use humor with love and respect.
- Listen actively.

Strange as it may sound, simply listening—with concern—is one of the best ways to build trust. "Just listening" can build a relationship. This concept is difficult for many mentors who understand the myriad tasks confronting their new teachers and want very much to tell them what works, to analyze, to question, to support. Often the new teacher needs encouragement, but in many cases these other kinds of help are not helpful at all.

"As a mentor project, I have held meetings for the new teachers at my school," one San Francisco mentor says (Jonson, 1999b). "Partly we focus on school activities such as an all-school writing test, but mostly the meetings are open-ended so the teachers can bring concerns and questions as well as stories of successes."

Ineffective mentors often have one or two styles of responses for most situations. Following are some typical ineffective ways of responding to problems.

Judging. The mentor might judge the mentee's thoughts or behaviors in some way. This judgment might be favorable (e.g., "That's a good idea," "You're on the right track now") or unfavorable ("An attitude like that won't get you anywhere"). In either case, the implication is that the mentor is superior and can pass judgment on the speaker's thoughts or actions. Furthermore, judgmental language is likely to make the beginning teacher defensive. This type of response might put the beginning teacher on guard and, in so doing, end the conversation and the possibility of help. "My mentee and I have a trusting relationship in that he can be open and honest when he needs to," one San Francisco mentor says. "He does not fear my judgment." (On the other hand, a mentor can help the beginning teacher evaluate and reflect on a situation in a nonjudgmental way.)

Analyzing. The analyzer's response suggests that the mentor understands the mentee better than the mentee does: "What's bothering you is . . ." or "What you really think is . . ." Two problems are associated with this sort of analyzing. First, the mentor's interpretation may not be correct, in which case the new teacher may become even more confused by accepting it. Second, even if the mentor's analysis is accurate, sharing it might not be useful to the mentee. It may make the mentee defensive (because analyzing implies superiority), or the beginning teacher may not be able to understand the mentor's view of the problem. Analyzing can be a way to help beginning teachers see the "blind parts" of themselves or a situation, but many mentors use this style of response too often and too early.

Questioning. Although questioning often helps mentors understand the unclear parts of a mentee's statements, it can also be used to direct the beginning teacher's thoughts. All beginning teachers have likely had the experience of being questioned by a parent, a teacher, or another authority figure who seemed to be trying to trap them. Used in this way, questioning implies that the person doing the asking already has some idea of what direction the discussion should take. The careful mentor will instead choose open-ended questions and will avoid questions that begin with "Why?"

Supporting. Sometimes the beginning teacher just needs encouragement, and a supportive response is the best thing in these cases. In many cases, however, this kind of response is not really much help. Telling an obviously upset beginning teacher that "everything is all right" or joking about a problem can communicate that the mentor does not accept the mentee's feelings or that the mentee's feelings are not justified.

Good intentions are not always enough. All of these responses may be helpful at times, but they often confuse those asking for help, making them feel defensive or worse than before they shared their problems. The mentor may be right about what caused the mentee's problem and how the mentee could solve the problem, but if beginning teachers do not discover the answer for themselves, it may not be useful to them. As one overzealous mentor commented, "[My mentee] often ignores the truth, even when it's so obvious you'd think she would trip over it."

Another way of responding can often be much more helpful. This style of response is simply active listening. With active listening, mentors maintain eye contact, ask questions to clarify, and otherwise help beginning teachers make clear their feelings. Mentors paraphrase beginning teachers' statements to check their understanding of what they hear, usually beginning by saying something like, "What I hear you telling me is . . ." In these kinds of conversations, it is important that mentors feed back only what they have heard the beginning teacher say without making any judgment or offering an interpretation. In building trust, the mentors' job is simply to understand, not to analyze or judge. Also, they should use their own language in checking back with the beginning teacher and not just parrot the original words.

To understand how listening can be so worthwhile, mentors need to realize that their role is really not to solve all their mentees' problems for them. Mentors can, however, help beginning teachers work things out for themselves. This is a difficult lesson for many mentors to learn. When someone they care for and are charged with supporting is in trouble and feeling bad, their first tendency is to try to make things better—to answer questions, soothe hurts, fix whatever is bothersome. Even in cases when mentors are sure they know what is right for the person, however, it is generally necessary to let that person discover the solution for him- or herself. Active listening is easy to implement, but its importance cannot be overemphasized in the development of mentor-mentee trust.

ADULT LIVES, ADULT LEARNING STYLES

> I need to understand Jean's whole life; I need to be able to see all the pressures on her. . . . I think we can work with the whole framework, the holistic approach, so that the chances of success are going to be greater than if we don't focus on the whole picture of the adult.
>
> —Laurent A. Daloz (1999, p. 110)

As mentors work with beginning teachers, they must keep in mind the whole of the beginning teacher's life. The temptation to "steer them into courses you know would be good for them without regard for their capacity to handle the work, given the rest of the forces in their lives" (Daloz, 1999, p. 110) is often great. Many of these beginning teachers are caught between duties at home/family relationships and the responsibilities of school/students' needs. They struggle to define new personal and professional lives. They are "learning to swim" in the give-and-take of whirling new roles. "It's a journey with a lot of potholes and trees across the road, and thunderstorms, and needing to take detours," one mentor explains. "Last term she really had to take a detour, and maybe she's had to fill in a couple of potholes this year, but she's underway again, still moving ahead" (Daloz, 1999, p. 109).

So what's a mentor to do? When facing difficult real-life challenges with her mentee, one mentor responded,

> Maybe just trying to be there with the flashlight and keeping the door at various places of the journey open when she wants or feels that she is able to make it in . . . helping her find balance, looking at the different piles of stuff in her life with the old flashlight and saying, "Where are you going to put this chunk called school?" (Daloz, 1999, p. 109).

Mentors must see themselves as facilitators of learning, all the while "listening, empowering, coaching, challenging, teaching, collaborating, aiding, assisting, supporting, expediting, easing, simplifying, advancing, and encouraging" (Zachary, 2000, p. 23). "Facilitators of learning see themselves as resources for learning rather than didactic instructors who have all the answers" (Brookfield, 1986, p. 63).

According to Brookfield (1986), "One important element in facilitating adult learning is helping learners become aware of their own idiosyncratic learning styles" (p. 64). Just as children have different learning preferences, patterns, or styles, so do adults. For some, learning through verbal modes is an easy and efficient method. These mentees learn best through their ears, picking up ideas more completely when they get or work with them auditorily. Others seem to grasp ideas more easily if they can see a diagram or a visual representation of what is being discussed. They are at their best when input comes through their eyes. For some, touch is especially important in their thinking and learning. Still others are kinesthetic learners and thinkers; motion and action are significant factors in how they interface with ideas. One mentor described her frustration working with a new teacher until the two of them began their conferences on the middle school playfield. Several times each week, they met on the playfield for a brisk walk around and around, with the young man pouring out his concerns as they pounded the track side by side. Only when the mentee was moving could he really express himself. Just as a child, then, so might the adult mentee benefit from learning strategies that take into account adult learning styles. Knowledge of these different learning styles, as well as of supervision models and stages in teacher development, can help mentors be more effective in their efforts.

Honoring specific learning styles helps facilitate learning. In her book, *The Mentor's Guide: Facilitating Effective Learning Relationships*, Lois Zachary (2000, pp. 24–25) offers further general guidelines that relate to adult learning styles or patterns of preferred responses:

- *Pace the learning.* The pace of learning varies and is often interrupted by individual need. Sometimes learners withdraw or become avoidant when they are uncomfortable. This self-declared time-out is part of the learning process as well and needs to be acknowledged.

- *Time the developmental intervention.* Mentors need to understand where their mentees are developmentally. They cannot assume readiness.
- *Keep the focus on learning.* Mentoring is not a chemistry contest. The partners should not get hung up on personality issues. Stick with the main attraction: learning.
- *Build the relationship first.* The learning will follow. Too often, mentors and mentees do not make the time to create the appropriate climate for learning.
- *Structure the process.* Sharing the responsibility for structuring the learning relationship (even in an informal learning relationship) improves the quality of the interaction.

In addition, it is always important that the mentor and mentee celebrate successes if the mentee is to remain engaged and enthusiastic. Success invites more success.

THE IMPORTANCE OF REFLECTION

Reflection is the fulcrum of learning that lasts. Without it, I doubt if protégés could sustain the changes we attempt to implement. Reflection provides distance so a protégé can look back at what has happened. The word reflection brings a mirror to mind. When we hold up a mirror, we can examine images in detail. Without it, we could have a distorted view or no view at all.

—Jane Fraser (1998, p. 55)

Whether it's student behavior or student writing, classroom relationships or classroom logistics, information from parents or information from administrators, the many issues that a teacher deals with throughout the day provide plenty of substance for reflection. To reflect, as *Merriam Webster's Collegiate Dictionary* (10th ed.) defines it, is "to think seriously; contemplate; ponder." Without such reflection, past events and occurrences disappear into history. Whether they have been dealt with well or not, they are done. With reflection on past events, though, they become stepping-stones to improvement, opportunities for growth. When teachers think about what they have learned from an experience, they can consolidate their knowledge and skills, evaluate their own performance, recognize successes, and develop strategies for improvement. For these reasons, reflecting on specific teaching problems as well as on larger professional and career development issues is important.

"In teaching, as in life, maximizing meaning from experiences requires reflection," write Costa and Kallick (2000).

The act of reflection, particularly with a group of teaching colleagues, provides an opportunity for the following:

- amplifying the meaning of one's work through the insights of others
- applying meaning beyond the situation in which it was learned
- making a commitment to modifications, plans, and experimentation
- documenting learning and providing a rich base of shared knowledge (Costa & Kallick, 2000, p. 60)

While reflection may seem to be a natural process, however, in fact, it is not. In a study of 42 preservice teachers at a Midwestern university, researchers found that those who received specific training in reflecting had significantly higher levels of reflection than did those in a control group. Notably, some who did not receive training improved their reflection skills anyway through repeated reflective exercises (Galvez-Martin, Bowman, & Morrison, 1999, p. 4). This study illustrates the need to work on the skill of reflection and to practice reflection regularly to realize its benefits.

Reflecting is at its most powerful when teachers collaborate in an active, honest search for answers. Perhaps the best way to reflect—the most productive—is out loud, talking with a mentor or a peer. Mentoring, in fact, is really just one teacher facilitating the growth of another. An active listener can be an important source of information for a beginning teacher, can provide emotional support, and often helps the beginning teacher grow and gain strength as a professional. Reflection should be a part of many of the teaching strategies discussed in Chapter 8: notably, demonstration teaching, observation and feedback, informal contact, and assistance with an action plan for professional growth.

Following interviews with 22 teacher-mentors in southern California, Shulman and Colbert reported that the mentors "suggested that teaching teachers how to reflect on their own teaching is what mentoring should ultimately include, because it will engender teachers with a mode for life-long improvement and revitalization" (Shulman & Colbert, 1988, p. 9).

Life can only be understood backwards; but it must be lived forwards.

—Søren Kierkegaard (quoted in Costa & Kallick, 2000, p. 60)

CONCLUSION

A teacher talented in working with children may not necessarily have the skills to work well with teachers as adults. This chapter reviewed different aspects of working with adult teachers: models of supervision used through the years, phases in the developing mentor-mentee relationship, the need to build a trusting relationship, and the importance of reflection. In Chapter 7, Stages in Teacher Development, we look at phases of growth specific to teachers and how mentors can shape their guidance of new teachers with those stages in mind.

> I needed these two years of support, having the time to deal with problems and being able to see myself in the "stages of development" for a beginning teacher as I ride the roller coaster through the depths of despair in December and January and then go back uphill toward the end of the year.
>
> —Cathy, a beginning teacher ("Teacher Voices," 1996, p. 3)

7

Stages in Teacher Development

I was elated to get the job but terrified about going from the simulated experience of student teaching to being the person completely in charge.

—A teacher in the stage of anticipation

I thought I'd be busy, something like student teaching, but this is crazy. I'm feeling like I'm constantly running. It's hard to focus on other aspects of my life.

—A teacher in the stage of survival

I thought I'd be focusing more on curriculum and less on classroom management and discipline. I'm stressed because I have some very problematic students who are low academically, and I think about them every second my eyes are open.

—A teacher in the stage of disillusionment

I'm really excited about my writing center, although the organization of it has at times been haphazard. Story writing has definitely revived my journals.

—A teacher in the stage of rejuvenation

I think that for next year I'd like to start the letter puppets earlier in the year to introduce the kids to more letters.

—A teacher in the stage of reflection

Teachers can generally be counted on to talk about developmental needs and stages when they discuss children. It may be meaningful to think of teachers themselves as having developmental sequences in their professional growth patterns as well. At the Santa Cruz New Teacher Center, researchers found that beginning teachers move through several developmental stages within their first year of teaching—from anticipation, to survival, to disillusionment, to rejuvenation, to reflection, and back to anticipation. In another model, Lilian Katz describes the developmental stages of teachers over the course of their career. Katz's model begins with the stage of survival and moves through consolidation to renewal and then to maturity. It is often helpful for the mentor to learn to recognize the particular stages new teachers go through and to adapt to the new teacher's needs. This understanding gives mentors a framework to design support that can make the mentee's first year of teaching a more positive experience.

THE FIRST YEAR: THE NEW TEACHER CENTER MODEL

After supporting some 1,500 new teachers, leaders of the Santa Cruz New Teacher Project noted several developmental phases common to beginning teachers (see Figure 7.1). Although not all teachers go through the phases in exactly the same sequence or timeframe, most follow the pattern to some degree (Moir, "Phases of First-Year Teaching"). Those working with new teachers may benefit from understanding these phases.

Anticipation

This first phase of teacher development precedes the teacher's first assignment, occurring at the end of student teaching during preservice training. Beginning teachers become excited and anxious about their pending assignments and may romanticize the role they will fill. They enter their own classroom for the first time with a sense of idealism and excitement that may carry them through the first few weeks of school.

Survival

Within the first month, the amount of material to be learned may quickly overwhelm new teachers. Despite their preparation and the anticipation they felt in the beginning, the reality of the job may catch them off-guard.

Figure 7.1   Phases of first-year teachers' attitudes toward teaching

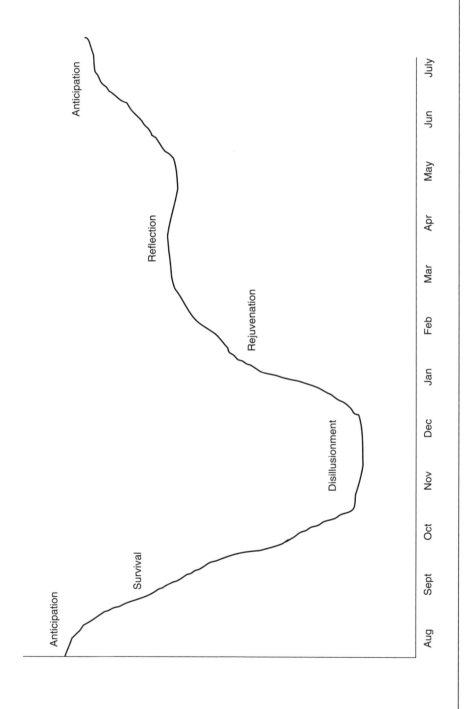

SOURCE: From *Attitudinal Phases of New Teacher Development*, by E. Moir. Retrieved from www.btsa.ca.gov/ba/profdev/princ_orient/docs/2-04.doc. Copyright by Ellen Moir. Reprinted with permission.

Day-to-day routines take all of their time, leaving little room for reflection. Beginning teachers may spend 70 hours a week just trying to keep up. Even in their exhaustion, though, they may remain energetic and committed, hoping that things will get easier.

Disillusionment

After six to eight weeks of hard work and nonstop stress, new teachers begin to lose energy and to question their commitment to the profession. Extensive demands on their time and discouragement may lead teachers to question their competence as they enter the phase of disillusionment. Back-to-school night, teacher conferences, and initial teacher evaluations all add to the stress, compounded sometimes by complaints from family members and friends about the excessive amount of time spent in teaching. Teachers experience self-doubt, have low self-esteem, and question their own professional commitment. Classroom management becomes a primary area of focus. Often teachers become ill during this time. "Getting through this phase may be the toughest challenge [new teachers] face," according to Moir ("Phases of First-Year Teaching").

Rejuvenation

Usually around January, after winter break, new teachers' attitudes begin to improve. They have been able to spend some time with family and friends during the holiday and to get proper rest, food, and exercise, possibly for the first time since beginning the school year. They have had a chance to organize their materials and plan lessons and are beginning to understand and accept the realities of teaching. Many new teachers have learned coping strategies and skills during the first half of the year and are better able to manage. Now they can focus on the business of curriculum development, long-term planning, and teaching strategies.

The phase of rejuvenation often lasts into the spring, with ups and downs throughout. Toward the end of the phase, new teachers may begin to wonder whether they will be able to accomplish everything necessary by the end of the school year and whether their students will be able to perform on tests. Just how effective has their teaching been?

Reflection

Beginning in about May, first-year teachers enter an invigorating phase of reflection. Looking back over the year, they think about their successes and about the things they did that were not so successful. They begin to plan things they will do differently next year: different methods of management, ways of presenting curriculum, and teaching strategies. From here, they circle back to anticipation as they look forward to the next year.

An understanding of these phases is critical in designing support systems for new teachers and offering mentoring services. While the teacher going through the survival mode may need support and help mostly with management, one in rejuvenation may be more interested in curriculum development. With an understanding of this common sequence, the mentor can tailor guidance to be most meaningful.

THROUGH THE YEARS: THE KATZ MODEL

In another model, Katz (1972) describes the developmental stages that teachers go through over time, which are generally linked to experience. Katz describes these stages as survival, consolidation, renewal, and maturity. Individual teachers vary greatly in the length of time spent in each of the stages outlined here, Katz says, but most progress through all four. This section outlines the four stages as described by Katz, with comments regarding developmental tasks and training needs for each stage.

Because mentoring and training needs change as mentors gain experience, a basic understanding of these stages may shape the assistance a mentor provides. See Figure 7.2 for teacher training needs at various developmental stages.

Figure 7.2   Training needs of teachers at different developmental stages

Developmental Stages	Training Needs
Stage IV	Seminars, institutes, courses, degree programs, books, journals, conferences
Stage III	Conferences, professional associations, journals, magazines, films, visits to demonstration projects
Stage II	On-site assistance, access to specialists, colleague advice, consultants
Stage I	On-site support and technical assistance
	0 1YR. 2YR. 3YR. 4YR. 5YR.

SOURCE: Katz, Lilian G. (2005). *The developmental stages of teachers*. Champaign, IL: Clearinghouse on Early Education and Parenting, University of Illinois at Urbana Champaign. Retrieved July 25, 2007, from http://ceep.crc.uiuc.edu/pubs/katz-dev-stages.html.

Survival

The first stage of teacher development according to Katz is the same as one of the early stages in the Santa Cruz model: survival. In Katz's model, this stage often lasts throughout the first full year of teaching.

Developmental Tasks. During the stage of survival, teachers' main concern is whether or not they can endure. They may ask such questions as, "Can I get through the day in one piece? Without losing my patience, my temper, my ideals? Can I make it until the end of the week—the next vacation? Can I really do this kind of work day after day? Will my colleagues accept me?"

The first full impact of responsibility for a group of immature but energetic students provokes teacher anxieties; approaching encounters with parents add to the stress. Discrepancies between anticipated success and classroom reality intensify feelings of inadequacy and unpreparedness.

Mentoring Needs. During the period of survival, teachers need support, understanding, encouragement, reassurance, comfort, and guidance. They need instruction in specific skills and insight into the complex causes of behavior—all at the classroom site. On-site mentoring must be constantly and readily available from someone who knows well both the trainee and the teaching situation. The mentor should have enough time and flexibility to be on call as needed by the trainee. Schedules of periodic visits that are arranged in advance cannot be counted on to coincide with the mentee's crises.

Consolidation

The second stage in Katz's model may begin late in the first year or early in the second year of teaching and often lasts into the beginning of the third year.

Developmental Tasks. By the end of their first year, teachers have usually decided that they are capable of surviving. They are ready to consolidate the overall gains made during the first stage and to differentiate specific tasks and skills to be mastered next. During the consolidation stage, teachers often begin to focus on individual problem students and problem situations. They look for answers to such questions as, "How can I help an inattentive child? How can I help a particular student who does not seem to be learning?"

During the stage of consolidation, the new teacher acquires a baseline of information about what students are like and what to expect of them. The teacher begins to identify individual students whose behavior departs from the pattern of most of the children.

Mentoring Needs. During the consolidation stage, on-site mentoring continues to be valuable. A mentor can help the teacher through mutual exploration of a problem. Take, for example, the case of a young elementary school teacher who was eager to get help and expressed her problem in the question, "How should I deal with a clinging child?" An on-site mentor could observe the teacher and child in the situation and suggest possible solutions fairly quickly. Without firsthand knowledge of the child and context, however, the mentor might best help the teacher interpret the experience and move toward a solution to the problem through an extended give-and-take conversation. The mentor might ask the teacher such questions as, "What have you done so far? Give an example of some experiences with this particular child during this week. When you did such and such, how did the child respond?"

Also in this stage, a wider range of resources might be necessary to help the new teacher gain information about specific students. Psychologists, social and health workers, and other specialists can strengthen the teacher's skills and knowledge during this stage. Exchanges of information and ideas with more experienced colleagues may help teachers master the developmental tasks of the period. Opportunities to share feelings with other teachers in the same stage of development may help reduce some of the teacher's sense of personal inadequacy and frustration.

Renewal

Katz's third stage of development often occurs during the third and fourth years of teaching.

Developmental Tasks. During the renewal stage, teachers begin to tire of doing the same old things. They start to ask more questions about new developments in the field: "Who is doing what? Where? What are some of the new materials, techniques, approaches, and ideas?" Although what they have been doing for each annual group of students may have been adequate, they find the recurrent Valentine cards, Easter bunnies, and pumpkin cutouts insufficiently interesting. If it is true that the interest and commitment of teachers to their projects and activities contribute to their educational value, then their need for renewal and refreshment should be taken seriously.

Training Needs. During the renewal stage, teachers find it especially rewarding to meet colleagues from different programs both formally and informally. Teachers in this stage are receptive to experiences in regional and national conferences and workshops, and they profit from membership in professional associations and participation in their meetings. They widen the scope of their reading, scan numerous magazines and journals, and view films. They may be ready to take a close look at their own classroom teaching through videotaping. This is also a time when teachers welcome opportunities to visit other classes, programs, and demonstration projects. The teacher center, designed to help teachers increase skills, may have the greatest potential value during this stage. Here teachers gather to help each other learn or relearn skills, techniques, and methods; to exchange ideas; and to organize special workshops. From time to time, specialists are invited to the center to meet with teachers and discuss curriculum, child growth, or other areas of concern for teachers.

Maturity

The fourth and final stage of teacher development in Katz's model might begin as early as the third year but often starts after five or more years.

Developmental Tasks. Teachers who have reached the stage of maturity have come to terms with themselves as teachers. They have enough perspective to begin to ask deeper and more abstract questions, such as "What are my historical and philosophical roots? What is the nature of growth and learning? How are educational decisions made? Can schools change societies? Is teaching a profession?" Perhaps they have asked these questions before, but with their greater experience, the questions now represent a more meaningful search for insight, perspective, and realism.

Training Needs. Throughout the maturity stage, teachers need opportunities to participate in conferences and seminars and perhaps to pursue other educational goals. Mature teachers welcome the chance to read widely and to interact with educators working on problem areas at many different levels. Training sessions and conference events enjoyable to teachers in the consolidation stage may be tiresome to the mature teacher. Teachers in this last stage, on the other hand, might enjoy introspective and searching discussion seminars that would lead to restlessness and irritability among teachers early in the survival stage.

CONCLUSION

It is often said that experience is the best teacher. Even so, we cannot assume that experience teaches what the new teacher should learn. One major goal of the teacher-mentor should be to direct learning, to try to make sure that the beginning teacher has informed and interpreted experience. Understanding the different phases of growth for teachers—through the first year and beyond—can help the mentor support and guide the beginner in meaningful ways. This chapter has looked at these various phases.

Chapter 8, Practical Strategies for Assisting New Teachers, looks at specific ways for mentors to help their new teachers develop professionally.

8

Practical Strategies for Assisting New Teachers

Karen Kawasaki, a new teacher at Mt. Carmel High School, "had great lesson plans, great ideas and projects, and an interactive style of teaching," according to Charlotte Kutzner, a veteran teacher in the Poway School District where Kawasaki teaches north of San Diego. But Kawasaki had a problem. As a new teacher, she also had trouble with classroom management, and after the school principal visited her classroom a couple of times, he told her that she needed to improve. She worried that she might lose her job.

In the Poway School District, teachers with two years or less of experience are assigned to teacher consultants. Unfortunately, Kawasaki's consultant had been out on sick leave. In November, a new consultant—Kutzner—was assigned.

"I was in her classroom once or twice a week," says Kutzner. "We talked a lot. We observed veteran teachers to see how they dealt with the problem. We even role-played ideas for how to handle students at the beginning of the class."

"Charlotte helped me a lot," Kawasaki says. "She made suggestions. . . . My confidence level went up."

At the end of the year, Kawasaki's job was assured, and she is now considered an excellent teacher.

—*California Teacher* (Bacon, 1997, pp. 1, 6)

Karen Kawasaki's situation was similar to that of many beginning teachers across the country: She was doing a lot right, but just couldn't figure out *everything* by herself. Unlike many beginning teachers, however, Kawasaki was fortunate enough to connect with an effective mentor who could guide her, who was available to her, and who was able to provide her with the quality time necessary for her to work through her problems at an appropriate pace (Fraser, 1998, p. 26). Charlotte Kutzner was able to be the kind of mentor Portner (1998, pp. 7–8) describes as ideal: one who can relate to new teachers' experiences, assess their abilities, coach them as they develop new skills, and guide them to reflect on their experiences.

"As consultants, we applaud what's going well, but also help teachers with their next best step," Kutzner says. "It's important to tailor assistance to the needs of the individual teacher" (Bacon, 1997, p. 7).

To get the most from their relationship, a mentor and a mentee need to plan together to determine goals that they will work toward. They should be realistic about the time they have and explicit about the things they want to work on (Stanulis & Weaver, 1998, p. 138). To help the beginning teacher reach these goals, the mentor must perform a variety of functions, ranging from observing in the classroom and providing feedback to helping the beginning teacher develop specific skills through serving as a role model in the full scope of daily professional activities (see Box 8.1).

BOX 8.1

Strategies a Good Mentor Can Use to Help the Beginning Teacher

- Share school protocol and traditions with the new teacher.
- Guide the mentee through the daily operation of the school.
- Explain school procedures as appropriate.
- Brainstorm with the mentee to help develop lesson plans.
- Provide occasional lesson plans.
- Suggest classroom management techniques.
- Role-play a parent conference.
- Examine student work together.
- Demonstrate lessons for the mentee.
- Demonstrate record keeping.
- Arrange for the mentee to visit a different teacher's classroom, and discuss the observation afterward; if time, join the new teacher during observation for later discussion.
- Observe the mentee's teaching and provide feedback.
- Meet regularly with the mentee, both formally and informally.
- Support and counsel the mentee, providing perspective when needed.
- Ask questions to help the beginning teacher prioritize issues and concerns.
- Assist the beginning teacher in developing an action plan for professional growth.
- Share resources, including materials for a curriculum unit, professional readings, children's literature, and so on.
- Attend a workshop together with the mentee.
- Role-model all aspects of professionalism.
- Encourage reflection.

Many of the strategies that experienced mentors find most helpful in aiding their mentees can be grouped into the following categories:

- Direct assistance
- Demonstration teaching
- Observation and feedback
- Informal contact
- Assistance with an action plan for professional growth
- Role modeling
- Assessing student work

A full description of each function follows. See Figure 8.1 for the range of mentor functions and Table 8.1 for the relative importance given to the first six functions by mentors surveyed in the San Francisco School District. No matter what the strategy, however, mentors should remember that the mentor-mentee relationship becomes more personally caring, and professional when their mentees perceive them as being genuinely interested—"helpful, caring, willing to take time, dedicated, friendly, outgoing, patient, influential" (Jonson, 1999b)—and as being professional role models.

Figure 8.1   Mentor functions

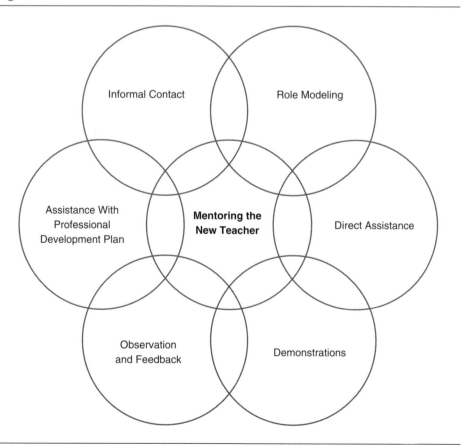

Table 8.1   The Importance of Mentoring Strategies

	Very Useful	Somewhat Useful	Not Useful	Not Practiced
Direct assistance	25	3	0	0
Demonstration teaching	18[a]	8	0	2
Observation and conferences	21[b,c]	5	0	2
Informal contact	24[d]	4	0	0
Assistance with professional growth plan	13	10	2	3
Role modeling	24[e,f]	3	1	0

SOURCE: Jonson (1999b).

NOTE: The following notes are quotes from the mentors surveyed.

a. When used to make a point.
b. If there is a trusting relationship.
c. If conferences are informal to minimize stress.
d. Informal contact may be several times/day . . . builds relationship and provides many quick "fixes" easily.
e. Useful if done before mentee takes over class. Less useful afterward because it dissipates mentee's position of authority in the eyes of the students.
f. The aspect of role modeling is not one I consciously set about doing. But, more than other areas, mentees tell me, in conversations several years later, that they wanted to "be like you." To me, it is a hidden part of mentoring. But, if the mentee doesn't feel that respect and admiration for the mentor, why would they pay attention to the mentor's ideas? I also think the respect other colleagues show for the mentor gives the mentee more reason to want to learn from the mentor.

DIRECT ASSISTANCE

> The new teacher looked distressed after school, so I engaged her in small talk for a few minutes. She then explained that a parent was giving her a hard time, and she asked me what to do about it. First, I had to let her know that it was the mother with the problem. I told her how I had handled similar problems and we came up with things she could do that are comfortable for her. She hasn't had any problems with that parent since then, but I believe she has a more positive self (teacher) image, and she feels more comfortable in dealing with unhappy parents.
>
> —A mentor (Jonson, 1999b)

Mentor-teachers carry out many specific tasks while helping beginning teachers. Various titles apply to these tasks: behaviors, functions, roles. Though some may fall under other categories of strategies as well, all involve the mentor giving assistance in some direct way.

Because beginning teachers want to achieve professional autonomy and status equality with their colleagues, a large percentage of them do not seek help from colleagues except indirectly by swapping stories about personal experiences. This behavior hides the weaknesses of beginners, but does not enable them to obtain help with those factors—inexperience, unavailability of expertise, and ambiguity about goal attainment—that produce teacher stress related to performing professional tasks.

Beginning teachers need practical suggestions for preventing problems, solving them when they occur, and resolving conflicts and other minor emergencies. Mentors who directly assist their mentees tend to be the most helpful. In fact, mentors in the San Francisco survey ranked direct assistance as being *very useful* more often than any other function (Jonson, 1999b).

In a classic study of first-year teachers in New York City, Sacks and Brady (1985) identified the following areas of need in which a mentor might directly assist a mentee:

- moral support, guidance, and feedback
- school routines and scheduling
- discipline and management
- curriculum and lesson planning
- individualized instruction
- motivational techniques

In addition, mentors often offer direct assistance to help the new teacher with career development.

Some mentors offer this help only when the mentee requests it; others step in whenever they see it as appropriate. Each mentor must personally decide when and how to offer direct assistance. Some mentees might see direct assistance as meddling or bossy—either because of the mentor's manner or because the mentee is not ready to receive help. But many are happy for the help. As one mentee in the Santa Cruz New Teacher Project advised new mentors, "Don't worry about being too direct. It's okay to give us specific suggestions. We don't always see what might not be working" (UCSC, 2003, p. 15).

"It helps if you can anticipate and help us prepare for events that are coming up, like reports," says another new teacher in the Oakland New Teacher Project. "Offer assistance in multiple forms—assessing for us or releasing us to assess. Meet for a useful period of time. Ten minutes is not enough" (UCSC, 2003, p. 15).

Recommended Procedures

Mentors need to offer to share the wealth of knowledge and experience they have gained but at the same time take care not to intimidate or overwhelm. It is important that the mentor make time available on a regular basis to address the mentee's concerns and progress and to ensure interaction. Sharing the same planning period helps a great deal. Box 8.2 lists a number of ways a mentor can directly assist a mentee.

BOX 8.2

Ways for a Mentor to Provide Direct Assistance

For moral support, guidance, and feedback:

- Respond to specific requests by mentees
- Encourage mentees in their efforts to develop their own ideas, teaching styles, and classroom management plans
- Encourage and support self-direction and autonomy
- Assist with room arrangement
- Model or suggest techniques for conferencing with parents
- Role-play a parent conference
- Act as a confidant for the mentee to express personal and professional concerns

With school routines and scheduling:

- Discuss written and unwritten rules, norms, and traditions in the school and community
- Assist in socializing within the school environment
- Give a tour of the district office and facilities
- Assist in filling out school forms
- Help the mentee develop and maintain a record-keeping system
- Identify resource people, such as the principal and staff development specialists in the district or in district and regional support agencies
- Explain school procedures regarding field trips

With discipline and management:

- Help the mentee develop a classroom management system
- Suggest options for classroom discipline
- Help the mentee develop a discipline plan

With curriculum and lesson planning:

- Help the mentee organize and manage materials
- Bring new methods, materials, and resources to the attention of the mentee and provide assistance in their implementation
- Provide examples of unit plans and course syllabi

- Co-plan an instructional unit or co-create a one-day lesson plan
- Co-develop a thematic unit
- Provide materials for a curriculum unit
- Brainstorm ways to introduce the curriculum unit
- Create materials together
- Suggest a strategy for reviewing literature
- Ask the new teacher how a strategy might affect student learning
- Point out gaps in lesson procedures
- Identify strengths in a lesson plan

With individualized instruction:

- Model skillful teaching strategies
- Confer with the mentee regarding effective ways to meet student learning objectives and district instructional goals
- Help the mentee diagnose students' learning styles and modify teaching strategies to meet all students' needs
- Arrange for the new teacher to observe another teacher
- Co-observe another teacher and discuss it afterward

With motivational techniques:

- Encourage the new teacher to try a new strategy
- Ask questions to help the new teacher prioritize issues related to instruction

With career development:

- Inform the mentee of workshops and other activities and opportunities for professional involvement
- Ask the new teacher to identify areas of strength and an area for professional growth
- Help the mentee assess current skills
- Ask questions to help the mentee self-assess
- Help the mentee identify specific competencies that need improvement
- Accompany the mentee for an evaluation conference with an administrator
- At the request of the mentee, assist in building competencies in areas of concern identified by the mentee's evaluator
- Assist the new teacher in developing a professional growth plan
- Help the new teacher select items to include in a portfolio
- Give feedback on the mentee's progress in meeting instructional goals

DEMONSTRATION TEACHING

A wealthy woman asked a famous millinery designer to design a hat for her. He placed a canvas form on her head, and in eight minutes with a single piece of ribbon, he created a beautiful hat right before her eyes. The matron was delighted. "How much will that be?" she asked. "Fifty dollars," he replied. "Why, that's outrageous," she said. "It's only a piece of ribbon!" The milliner quickly unraveled the ribbon and, handing it to her, said, "Madame, the ribbon is free!"[1]

A demonstration occurs when an experienced teacher shows a beginning teacher the proper use of a strategy, technique, or skill by incorporating it into an actual classroom lesson. One of the more important functions of a mentor-teacher is to prepare and teach demonstration lessons so that a mentee can observe specific techniques or materials being used. Often the beginning teacher can learn from watching how the mentor manages the class, presents curriculum, and deals with problems. At other times, the mentor might suggest that another teacher demonstrate a particular technique.

Videotapes, whether prepared locally or commercially, also can be used to demonstrate effective teaching. Videotapes offer some specific advantages, including convenience and consistency, but they cannot replace the effect of a live demonstration and subsequent conferences with the demonstrating teacher.

"Be willing to model lessons with the (new) teacher's class," a new teacher in the Santa Cruz New Teacher Project advises mentees. "It's neat to see what the advisor will do with my kids as things come up in a lesson" (UCSC, 2003, p. 15).

When to Use Demonstrations

Following are examples of appropriate times for demonstrations by a mentor-teacher:

- On request of the mentee
- After a mentor's observation of the mentee and identification of a technique that could be useful to the mentee
- By mutual agreement
- When the mentor has a specific technique to share
- On a regularly scheduled basis
- As part of the mentee's professional development plan

---

1. As seen in DEAR ABBY written by Abigail Van Buren a.k.a. Jeanne Phillips and founded by her mother, Pauline Phillips. © Universal Press Syndicate. Reprinted with permission. All rights reserved.

Recommended Procedures

A number of mentor/mentee teams have used the following procedure successfully when providing demonstration lessons (Jonson, 1999b).

- *Predemonstration conference.* The mentor and mentee determine the goal of the demonstration/observation and what the mentee should observe and record.
- *Demonstration.* The mentor demonstrates the preestablished lesson at the scheduled time while the mentee observes.
- *Postdemonstration conference.* The mentor and mentee review and analyze what was accomplished by the demonstration. In so doing, the mentor must remember that the idea is to help, not to threaten. The two then make plans for the mentee to practice the observed skill(s), for additional observations in the mentor-teacher's classroom, or both.

This procedure uses the pre- and postconference format advocated in the cognitive coaching model of Costa and Garmston (1994). See Chapter 6 for more information on cognitive coaching.

OBSERVATION AND FEEDBACK

> When she observed my teaching, my cooperating teacher would always offer feedback in a very positive way, even when it was critical. I never felt that what she said was threatening to me, or that sense of "Oh, no, she really hated what I did" or anything like that.
>
> —New teacher (Developmental Studies Center, 1998, p. 31)

The demanding pace of the classroom gives beginning teachers little time to monitor or reflect on their behavior. As a result, they tend to use automatic rather than deliberate responses to handle recurring classroom situations. A variety of studies in teacher expectations and attitudes, teacher-student relationships, student attitudes, and student learning progress have demonstrated that more effective teachers tend to be "proactive," that is, to assume and maintain the initiative in structuring classroom events. Less effective teachers tend to be more "reactive," lacking clarity of objectives and methods of reaching them and less "in charge" in their classrooms.

Observing the beginning teacher and providing feedback through a postobservation conference are important mentoring activities that can help beginning teachers. Research findings indicate that formal observation and feedback are especially effective for improving instruction (Costa & Garmston, 1994; Hunter, 1994; Showers, 1985). Feedback provided through written critiques, descriptions of classroom interaction analysis, behavior analysis, self-critiqued videotape, and other methods can also be helpful—but the use of a conference is preferred.

Feedback based on classroom observations makes beginning teachers aware of problems and helps bring about change. Sometimes the changes are obvious and simple to make, such as altering a physical arrangement in the classroom. Other changes are less obvious, and systematic feedback is needed to clarify the problem and explore ways to make appropriate changes. The mentor may find that several observation-feedback cycles are necessary to focus on the beginning teacher's patterns of calling on students and involving them in classroom discussions, for example. Additionally, the beginning teacher may need to be encouraged to attend specific professional development programs to make changes because the teaching skills are complex. In general, the value of the mentor's feedback depends on its quality and presentation. All feedback should

- address specific, concrete behaviors or characteristics;
- be focused, nonjudgmental, and evidence based;
- be credible and presented with caring intentions and in understandable terms;
- include specific guidelines for growth; and
- lead to a commitment to initiate new or expanded strategies.

When mentors observe a mentee, they must note specifically what the beginning teacher is doing, what is working well, and where guidance is needed. The idea is for mentors to record exactly what is seen and then share observations in a way that is productive and supportive. If possible, mentors should help the beginning teacher see which existing behaviors are successful and raise the possibility of extending those behaviors rather than switching to entirely new ones. Mentors must describe the problem(s), but allow for lots of input from the beginning teacher. Feedback conferences tend to be especially productive if the beginning teacher has jotted down questions for discussion before the conference (Developmental Studies Center, 1998, p. 31).

Observation and feedback can initially be uncomfortable for both parties. With a good, trusting, supporting relationship, however, the mentor and the mentee will be able to achieve their goals through this process. A beginning teacher in California who participated in an extensive observation process found the experience worthwhile—despite the fact that the process was rigorous, with the mentor collecting information before and during the observation, comparing the results with the state standards for the teaching profession, and sharing the results in great detail with new teachers:

> The greatest benefit for me [in the mentoring program] was to be observed by an objective party who was able to tell me the good things that I was doing and the areas where I could improve.

My observer affirmed my strengths but also helped me let myself "off the hook" of perfection. I allow myself to be in a learning process—like the children in my class.

—Laura Wong, new teacher (Schultz, 1999, p. 103)

When to Use Observation and Feedback

What are beginning teachers interested in having observed? When mentors ask their mentees what concerns them and what they would like the mentor to observe, record, and provide feedback about, teachers request information about two distinct categories of behaviors: their own and that of their students. Behaviors can further be classified as verbal or nonverbal. Tables 8.2 through 8.5 give examples of verbal and nonverbal behaviors that teachers often want mentors to observe in the classroom (Costa & Garmston, 1994, pp. 29–31).

Recommended Procedure: The Formal Conference

A formal observation-and-conference cycle follows steps similar to those described for demonstrations. In this case, though, the mentee is the focus of the observations discussed.

The formal mentor observation and conference has three parts:

1. Preobservation conference

2. Observation

3. Postobservation conference

Ideally, the mentor and the mentee engage in the formal observation-conferencing process at least once a month. They should remember that this is a collaborative decision-making process, with the mentor and the mentee discussing and agreeing on each point.

Preobservation Conference

The reliability and usefulness of a classroom observation relate directly to the amount and kind of information the observer has obtained beforehand (McGreal, 1983, p. 98). During the preconference, the mentor should gather information, and both mentor and mentee should determine a focus for the observation.

"I appreciate when my advisor is receptive to hearing my needs instead of having their own agenda," a new teacher in the Santa Cruz New Teacher Project says (UCSC, 2003, p. 15). "Help me with what I need rather than what we're supposed to do. . . . It's important for me to have a say in scheduling the time and focus of our meetings."

Table 8.2   Nonverbal Feedback Most Often Requested by Teachers About Themselves

Description	Example
A. Mannerisms	Pencil tapping, hair twisting, handling coins in pocket
B. Use of time	Interruptions; transitions from one activity to another; time spent with each group; time spent getting class started, dealing with routines (such as attendance), etc.; punctuality in starting/ending times
C. Movement throughout the classroom	Favoring one side of the classroom over another; monitoring student progress and seatwork
D. Modality preference	Using balanced visual, kinesthetic, and auditory modes of instruction
E. Use of handouts	Clarity, meaningfulness, adequacy, and/or complexity of seatwork
F. Use of AV equipment	Placement, appropriateness, operation
G. Pacing	Too fast, too slow, "beating a dead horse" (tempo/rhythm)
H. Meeting diverse student needs	Considering/making allowances for: gifted/challenged; cognitive styles; emotional needs; modality strengths; languages, cultures, etc.
I. Nonverbal feedback	Body language, gestures, proximity, eye contact; moving or leaning toward students when addressing them
J. Classroom arrangements	Furniture placement, bulletin board space, environment for learning, provision for multiple uses of space/activities

SOURCE: Costa, A. L., & Garmston, R. J. (1994). *Cognitive Coaching: A Foundation for Renaissance Schools* (p. 29). Norwood, MA: Christopher-Gordon Publishers.

Table 8.3   Verbal Feedback Most Often Requested by Teachers About
Themselves

Description	Example
A. Mannerisms	Saying "okay," "you know," or other phrases excessively
B. Sarcasm/negative feedback	Gender references; criticism; put-downs; intonations
C. Positive/negative feedback	Use of praise, criticism, ignoring distracting student responses
D. Response behaviors	Silence, accepting, paraphrasing, clarifying, empathizing; responding to students who give "wrong" answers
E. Questioning strategies	Posing taxonomical levels of questions; asking questions in sequences
F. Clarity of presentation	Giving clear directions, making assignments clear, checking for understanding, modeling
G. Interactive patterns	Teacher—>Student—> Teacher—>Student Teacher—>Student—> Student—>Student
H. Equitable distribution of responses	Favoring gender, language proficiency, culture, perception of abilities, placement in room, etc.
I. Specific activities/teaching strategies	Lectures, group activities, lab exercises, discussion videos

SOURCE: Costa, A. L., & Garmston, R. J. (1994). *Cognitive Coaching: A Foundation for Renaissance Schools* (p. 29). Norwood, MA: Christopher-Gordon Publishers.

Table 8.4   Nonverbal Feedback Most Often Requested by Teachers About Their Students

Description	Example
A. Attentiveness	On task/off task, note taking, volunteering for tasks
B. Preparedness	Participation, sharing, homework, materials, volunteering knowledge
C. Movement	Negative: out of seat, squirming, fidgeting, discomfort, interfering with others
	Positive: following directions, transitioning, self-direction, taking initiative, consulting references/atlases/dictionaries, etc.
D. Managing materials	AV equipment, textual materials, art supplies, musical instruments, lab equipment, care of library books, returning supplies, etc.

SOURCE: Costa, A. L., & Garmston, R. J. (1994). *Cognitive Coaching: A Foundation for Renaissance Schools* (p. 29). Norwood, MA: Christopher-Gordon Publishers.

Acheson and Gall (1980, p. 98) suggest the following agenda for determining goals during a preconference. They also recommend following these steps in order. By doing so, they say, mentor and mentee together identify the teacher's concerns about instruction.

1. Translate the teacher's concerns into observable behaviors

2. Identify procedures for improving the teacher's instruction

3. Assist the teacher in setting self-improvement goals

4. Arrange a time for classroom observation

5. Select an observation instrument and behaviors to be recorded

6. Clarify the instructional context in which data will be recorded

The emphasis for the observation is on collecting data regarding matters of interest to the beginning teacher. Use the preconference log in Figure 8.2 to help organize the procedure and focus for observation of the new teacher.

Table 8.5   Verbal Feedback Most Often Requested by Teachers About Their Students

Description	Example
A. Participating	Positive: volunteering verbal responses, speaking out—on task, student-to-student interaction—on task, requesting assistance
	Negative: speaking out—off task, student-to-student interaction—off task
B. Social interaction	Positive: listening, allowing for differences, sharing, establishing ground rules, assuming and carrying out roles, following rules of games, etc.
	Negative: interrupting, interfering, hitting, name calling, put-downs, culturally insensitive language, swearing, hoarding, stealing
C. Performing lesson objectives	Using correct terminology; applying knowledge learned before or elsewhere; performing task correctly; conducting experiments; applying rules, algorithms, procedures, formulas, etc.; recalling information; supplying supportive details, rationale, elaboration
D. Language patterns	Using correct grammar, spelling, punctuation, counting; using correct syntax; supplying examples
E. Insights into student behaviors/difficulties	Learning styles: verbal, auditory, kinesthetic, etc.; cognitive styles: field sensitive, field independent, etc.; friendships/animosities; tolerance for ambiguity/disorder; distractibility

SOURCE: Costa, A. L., & Garmston, R. J. (1994). *Cognitive Coaching: A Foundation for Renaissance Schools* (p. 29). Norwood, MA: Christopher-Gordon Publishers.

First Observation

Observation in this case does not mean simply watching; rather, it means intentionally and methodically observing interaction between the teacher and students. It should be planned, careful, focused, and active. Once the focus has been determined at the preconference, the mentor needs to keep

Figure 8.2   Preconference log

Preconference Log (to be filled out by member)

Date of preconference: _____

Teacher: _____

Mentor: _____

Lesson background:

- What subject will the teacher be teaching when observed?
- What is the purpose of the lesson that will be observed?

Observation:

- What is the reason and purpose for the observation?
- What is the specific focus of the observations?
- How will the observation be recorded?

Date of observation: _____

Location of observation: _____

Time of observation: _____

Date of postconference: _____

Location of postconference: _____

Time of postconference: _____

SOURCE: From Appendix A (p. 110) in *Leadership for Learning: How to Help Teachers Succeed,* by Carl D. Glickman—Alexandria, VA; ASCD, 2002. Used with permission. The Association of Supervision and Curriculum Development is a worldwide community of educators advocating sound policies and sharing best practices to achieve the success of each learner. To learn more, visit ASCD at www.ascd.org.

that focus during the observation. The more narrowly the mentor is able to focus, the more accurate will be the classroom observation (McGreal, 1983, p. 102). The mentor also needs to record data during the observation to be recalled later in a postconference. Several techniques for recording data are discussed under the heading "Tools for Observation," later in this chapter.

Postobservation Conference

During this last phase of the observation-and-conference cycle, the mentor provides feedback to help the mentee improve. The idea is for the mentor to describe what has been observed, not to pass judgment. Any feedback should be in strict confidence; in most districts, the mentor is not part of the system of teacher evaluation and avoids discussing the performance of the beginning teacher with other staff. Inexperienced mentors, being quite proud of their data-gathering ability and having worked hard during the observation to take notes, may be eager to tell the beginning teacher everything they have seen. Doing so, however, will make it impossible for the beginning teacher to process all of the information. Costa and Garmston (1994) offer the following tips on data reporting to help avoid this common problem:

- Sit side by side with the mentee so that the mentee can see the mentor's notes.
- Begin by having the *mentee* recollect the lesson. This gives the mentor something to build on and also helps the mentee develop self-reflecting and self-coaching skills.
- If the mentee introduces important but tangential problems or concerns during the postconference, deal with them briefly—but don't abandon the originally planned discussion. Keeping focus enables the mentor to manage time.
- Give the mentee notes to have. In some cases, it might even help to give the mentee notes *before* the postobservation meeting.

Offering feedback in positive terms will enhance trust and support and will reduce anxiety. But it is also important for feedback to be honest. "If mentors are unwilling to criticize," writes Glenn, "perhaps out of fear of negatively affecting the relationship . . . progress will be slow in coming. Unless . . . teachers know where their areas for improvement lie, they are likely to flounder with no direction" (2006, p. 91).

The following guidelines will help the mentor provide positive but constructive feedback:

- Focus feedback on the behavior, rather than on the person
- Provide objective feedback, and cite specific examples
- Describe rather than judge
- Point out specific causes and effects
- Share ideas rather than give advice
- Explore alternatives, rather than give solutions
- Give only the amount of feedback the receiver can use
- Provide feedback valuable for the receiver, rather than for the giver

It is important to keep the focus on the topic determined in the preobservation conference. Without such a focus, the discussion is likely to move to issues outside the classroom, away from the goal of improving learning for students (Glickman, 2002, p. 35).

Second and Subsequent Observations and Conferences

Mentors and mentees will require more than one observation-and-conference sequence to establish a strong, trusting relationship. Once this level of trust has been achieved, the mentor and the beginning teacher are ready to proceed to other observations and conferences focused on specific instructional growth for the beginning teacher. This process of preconference, observation, and postconference should continue throughout the year, changing focus as the needs of the beginning teacher change. See Box 8.3 for helpful guidelines.

BOX 8.3

Guidelines to Help a Mentee in Subsequent Observations and Conferences

Preobservation Conference (5–10 minutes)

- Set dates and times for the observation and postconference
- Determine what the mentee would like to have observed
- Determine where the observer is to sit in the class
- Discuss the lesson plan and material to be taught
- Specify the observation tools to be used (see next section)

Observation (20–50 minutes)

- Observe one or two teaching behaviors or strategies
- Use the observation form agreed on in the preconference

Postobservation Conference (10–30 minutes)

- Set a relaxed tone
- Discuss objective data, not viewpoints or judgments
- Explore strategies, alternatives, causes, and effects
- Discuss areas of focus for future observations and other activities

---

Tools for Observation

Using observation tools is like taking snapshots of classroom events.

The purpose is to record, in an objective and usable manner, the verbal and nonverbal behaviors of students and teachers. Many types of observation tools exist; following are some examples. Mentors and their mentees are encouraged to use whatever observation tools and techniques they agree will be helpful or to develop their own.

Seating Charts

Several techniques for observing student and teacher behaviors make use of the seating chart format. These techniques have several advantages:

- They are easy to use and interpret.
- A large body of information can be recorded on a single chart.

- They deal with relatively important aspects of classroom behavior.
- They enable the observer to record one student's behavior while at the same time observing the teacher and the class as a whole.

1. *Student/Teacher Question Patterns.* A seating chart can be used to record the frequency of each student's interaction with the teacher during a question-and-answer session.

Directions. When the teacher asks an individual student a question, place an arrow in that student's box on the seating chart. The arrow should be pointing away from the teacher. Each subsequent question directed to that student should be marked with a slash through the same arrow. In Figure 8.3, one student was asked two questions, and the other student was asked four questions.

Figure 8.3   Question patterns: Teacher to individual student

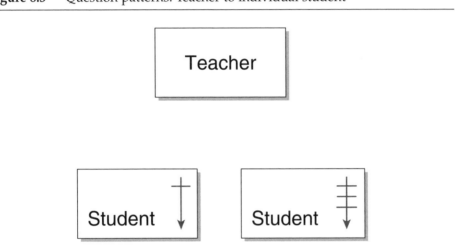

When the teacher directs questions to the entire class, place an arrow in or near the teacher's box on the classroom map/seating chart (see Figure 8.4). The arrow should point in the direction of the class. Subsequent questions directed to the entire class should be recorded as slash marks through the same arrow.

When a student asks a question or responds to the teacher's question, place an arrow in or near that student's box on the seating chart (see Figure 8.5). In this instance, the arrow should point toward the teacher. Subsequent questions and responses by the student should be marked by slashes through the same arrow.

2. *On-Task Behavior.* A seating chart or classroom map is useful for providing data on whether students are engaged in appropriate, "on-task" behavior at specified times during a lesson or activity.

Figure 8.4   Question patterns: Teacher to entire class

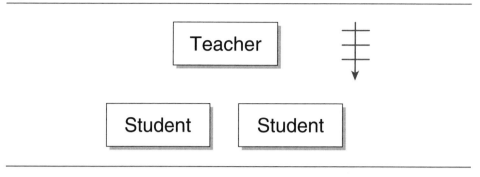

Figure 8.5   Question patterns: Student to teacher

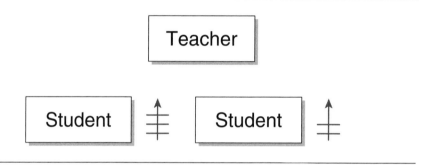

Directions. Observe the class at three- or five-minute intervals. Using the agreed-on behavior categories, note what each student is doing at the specified times, and mark the appropriate symbols in the student's box. In Figure 8.6, two students were chatting with others (i.e., were off task) at 9:00, but all students were on task at 9:03.

3. *Reinforcement and Feedback.* A seating chart may also be used to record teacher responses to individual student behavior. An observer/ mentor (with the beginning teacher's agreement) may wish to learn whether the beginning teacher's communications with the class (or with an individual student) are predominantly positive, for example.

Directions. Each time the teacher provides feedback to an individual student, decide whether the feedback is a reprimand, a positive response (such as a compliment or affirmation), a correction, or a neutral response. Then place the symbol for that feedback in the student's box (see Figure 8.7).

4. *Classroom Movement Patterns.* The observer/mentor and the beginning teacher may be interested in recording teacher and/or student movement around the classroom during a period of time. Data on a seating

Figure 8.6   On-task behavior

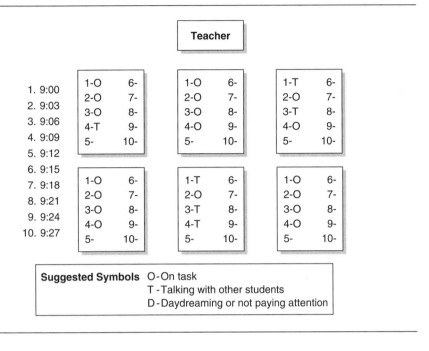

Figure 8.7   Reinforcement and feedback

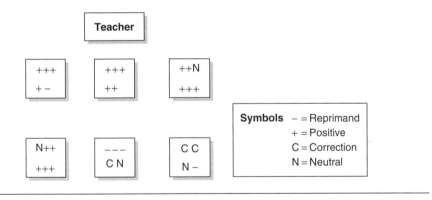

chart or classroom map may provide information concerning teacher bias, classroom management procedures, student engagement, or some other aspect of classroom behavior.

Directions. Use lines with arrows to show which students move about the room during the observation period (see Figure 8.8).

Draw lines with arrows to record *teacher* movement during the observation (see Figure 8.9).

Figure 8.8   Student movement patterns

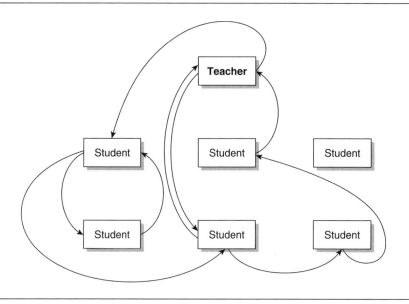

Figure 8.9   Teacher movement patterns

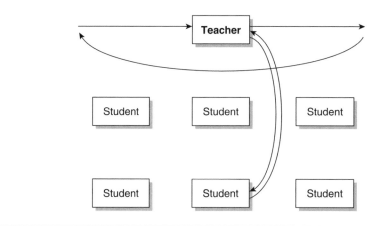

5. *Cause-and-Effect Records.* This observation tool is designed to give the observer/mentor and the beginning teacher information concerning the influence of the teacher's actions on student response in the classroom. It can be useful for observing a teacher's classroom management, questioning strategies, direction giving, and other behaviors that call for a student response.

Directions. Divide a blank sheet of paper into two columns. Record teacher actions in the left-hand column and student response to these actions in the right-hand column (see Figure 8.10).

Figure 8.10   Cause-and-effect record

Teacher	Student (response)
Bell	Students moving to their seats
Roll taken	Students talking quietly to each other
Surveys class	Room quiets down
Teacher turns on overhead and says, "Take out a piece of paper and answer the following questions about yesterday's reading assignment."	Students look at overhead and some students begin to take out paper

6. *Verbatim Transcripts.* Many mentors and supervisors have been trained to use an exact written record of teacher-and-student verbal interactions during an observation period. Whether it is selective (i.e., whether the kinds of verbal events to be recorded have been decided on beforehand) or a complete account of teacher-and-student verbal behavior, the verbatim transcript allows for a rather thorough analysis of what has transpired in the classroom during the observation. Many experts advocate the use of the verbatim transcript because of its specificity in providing the beginning teacher with feedback.

7. *Videotapes.* Videotaping a lesson for the mentor and the beginning teacher to review together later can also provide valuable information. This is especially helpful if the camera is set up to catch student body language and facial expressions. In this way, both participants can "observe" the lesson together during the feedback cycle.

INFORMAL CONTACT

"I didn't even think of this until we started talking about it today," a first-year teacher in middle school language arts professed to her mentor one day as the two conversed. "Oh, now that makes sense when I hear myself saying it," she said another time. Yet a third time, she exclaimed, "I feel like the sun's come out! I know this is the way we need to go."

—"Kelly," first-year middle school teacher
(Stanulis & Weaver, 1998, p. 136)

In their report of the study involving this inexperienced teacher, Stanulis and Weaver (1998) write, "In setting aside the time to talk, we were honoring one of the primary ways in which teachers do business and make meaning: talking about issues and problems with a colleague" (p. 136).

In fact, informal contact, the easiest form of assistance to provide, may also be the most helpful overall. Beginning teachers and mentors frequently state that informal discussions with experienced teachers are the most valuable type of assistance. The beginning teacher needs to know about so many "nuts and bolts"—but doesn't. Even the policies and procedures that *are* explained in preservice orientation often are forgotten in the excitement of the new school year. A bit of information, some timely suggestions, or a few words of understanding and encouragement can be a big help.

Effective mentors make a point of visiting their mentees and generally being around, especially during the first few days of school. In fact, when asked to list qualities in a good mentor, one respondent to the survey of San Francisco mentors noted simply, "being *available* to the mentee for discussions, exploration, etc." (Jonson, 1999b). Close physical proximity between the mentor's and the mentee's classrooms is highly desirable to facilitate informal contact. This allows the mentor to meet informally but frequently with the beginning teacher to discuss such day-to-day concerns as

- taking attendance,
- understanding school discipline policies,
- acquiring supplies and materials,
- planning classroom instruction,
- coping with daily problems, and
- understanding contracts and benefits.

Any concerns of beginning teachers are valid subjects for frequent informal conferences. Consequently, the mentor should make an effort to be both available and easily accessible to the beginning teacher, especially during the first few weeks of the school year.

ASSISTANCE WITH AN ACTION PLAN FOR PROFESSIONAL GROWTH

An important premise of coaching shared by other promising practices is the view of professional growth as ongoing learning. Conditions necessary for the professional growth of teachers parallel essential ingredients of adult development. Educators, like all adult learners, need the autonomy to direct and take responsibility for their own learning. (Levine, 1989, p. 243)

One important key to successful mentoring is moving the mentee from some level of dependence on the mentor-teacher to a high level of self-direction. As a logical step in this process, the mentee can begin to plan, formally or informally, a professional development process. In several states, in fact, new teachers must come up with a Professional Development Plan during their first year to be implemented over the next three to five years to qualify for a renewable license. This process is separate from any evaluation of the mentee and can follow the processes of observation, demonstration, coaching, and reflection.

Mentors must be conscious of how their own professional development serves as a model for their mentees. Lifelong learning is as much an attitude as an activity. It is a way of life for professionals.

Many kinds of professional planning assistance are possible. The mentor-teacher can assist in planning professional development by doing the following:

- Sharing views concerning possible career paths and goals
- Providing direct assistance: answering questions, suggesting strategies, supplying resources
- Creating opportunities for mentees to become involved in professional activities—such as faculty activities, professional associations, special projects—and to "prove" themselves as professionals
- Providing information on the mentor's own professional development plan as a model
- Assisting the mentee in setting short- and long-term professional goals
- Acting as a resource to help the mentee obtain information such as certification and continuing education requirements
- Suggesting or providing books, articles, professional videos, and so on

Appendix B contains sample forms that a mentor might review with a mentee to help the mentee define goals for growth. A good plan should do the following:

1. Clarify the *roles and responsibilities* of the mentor and mentee

2. Provide a *focus and framework* for mentor-mentee teamwork

3. Become an *informative resource* when shared with others

Goals should be short-term, achievable within a few months. Plans should be revisited and revised or rewritten two or three times per year so that the beginning teacher can gain a sense of accomplishment and growth.

In addition, the mentor should be sensitive to the beginning teacher's own agenda for professional development. Many beginning teachers are as busy as they can be just filling the requirements of maintaining their credentials. Some work to complete a master's degree in the first year or two while on the job. Any other plans for development should be coordinated with these activities.

ROLE MODELING

The aspect of role modeling is not one I consciously set about doing. But, more than in other areas, mentees tell me in conversations several years later that they wanted to "be like [me]." To me, that is a hidden part of mentoring. But if the mentee doesn't feel that respect and admiration for the mentor, why would he pay attention to the mentor's ideas? I also think the respect other colleagues show for the mentor gives the mentee more reason to want to learn from the mentor.

—A mentor (Jonson, 1999b)

Literature on mentoring emphasizes the importance of providing beginning teachers with role models for personal and professional behavior. What seems to confirm and enhance the mentoring relationship is the mentee's respect for the mentor as a professional and as a human being who is living a life worthy of that respect. In addition to helping the beginning teacher acquire skills and knowledge, the mentor-teacher must model a commitment to professional growth (see Box 8.4). Important to the mentoring relationship is not just what mentors *know*, but who they *are*.

BOX 8.4

The Mentor-Teacher as a Model

The mentor-teacher becomes a model:

- In relations with colleagues, students, parents, and others
- By demonstrating a commitment to student growth and development
- By demonstrating exemplary skills in the classroom
- In collaborative endeavors with other professionals (collegial interaction and support)
- In work habits
- By modeling a professional growth commitment and having a personal and professional development plan
- By active involvement in professional activities and professional organizations
- By seeking knowledge of trends in education, including new teaching materials, methodology, and research
- By expressing a positive set of values and beliefs concerning teaching as a career
- By being a facilitator of change and improvement

Role modeling means much more than the mentor doing demonstration teaching. It means exhibiting professionalism; it means showing the mentee how to get things done within the political climate of the school; it means demonstrating realistic ways of solving problems; it means exhibiting energy, self-confidence, security, and competency.

With the aid of an effective role model, the mentee develops a sense of professional identity and competence. The mentor, in turn, profits in the areas of technical and psychological support, internal satisfaction, and increased respect from colleagues (Kram, 1985).

ASSESSING STUDENT WORK

Is the work good? What is good?

In a survey of first-year teachers, Mandel asked what novices most want help with. High on the list was grading fairly (2006, p. 68). "They want the grades to be accurate, but not to hurt a student's self-esteem," Mandel writes. "Efficient and fair grading, one of the most fundamental teacher tasks, is not a skill normally taught in education classes or new teacher workshops. Somehow, our education system seems to assume that new teachers already know effective grading techniques or can easily learn them on their own. But fair grading is complicated."

Writing, exams, projects, and portfolios all can be used to measure student achievement. Examining student work is a large part of every teacher's job, for two reasons: (1) Grades let students know how they are progressing and (2) they let teachers know how effective their instruction is. A good assessment of student work can help the teacher develop classroom instruction. In isolation, though, a new teacher may not have a clear context for assessment. Discussion with a colleague can help the new teacher focus and analyze the work on a broader scale.

Together, a mentor and mentee might assess several samples of work from one student, one assignment as completed by several students, or successful and less successful samples of a given assignment. Blythe, Allen, and Powell (1999, p. 10) suggest several questions to guide an assessment of student work. They relate to the work itself, teaching practice, student understanding, student growth, and student intent. For a list of these questions, see Box 8.5.

Recommended Procedures

Before meeting, mentees decide what they would like to learn from the assessment, select samples of student work for discussion, and prepare context information: a description of the assignment, the rubric, and so on. If appropriate, mentees make an extra copy of work so that they and their mentors can each have one.

BOX 8.5

Kinds of Questions to Guide the Examination of Student Work

About the quality of student work:

- Is the work good enough?
- What is good enough?
- In what ways does this work meet or fail to meet a particular set of standards? About teaching practice:
- What do the students' responses indicate about the effectiveness of the prompt or assignment?
- How might the assignment be improved?
- What kinds of instruction support high-quality student performances?

About the student's understanding:

- What does this work tell us about how well the student understands the topic of the assignment?
- What initial understanding do we see beginning to emerge in this work?

About the student's growth:

- How does this range of work from a single student demonstrate growth over time?
- How can I support student growth more effectively?

About the student's intent:

- What issues or questions is this student focused on?
- What aspects of the assignment intrigued this student?
- Which parts of the assignment called forth the most effort from the student?
- To what extent is the student challenging herself? In what ways?

Following a meeting on "Examining Student Work and School Change" in Chicago in October 1998 (hosted by the Chicago Learning Collaborative and the Annenberg Institute for School Reform), an association of individuals and educational organizations developed a Web site (www.lasw.org) focused on looking at student work to strengthen connections between student learning and instruction, curriculum, and other aspects of school life. The Web site gives suggestions for teachers looking together at student work and reflecting on important questions about teaching and learning. Although the focus is not on mentors working with mentees, many of the ideas are important and transferable. According to advice given on the Web site, the teacher bringing work for discussion (perhaps the mentee) should choose a particular focus for discussion. The question might be broad: *How can I support higher-quality presentations? What are the strengths and weaknesses in the student presentations?* Or the focus might be narrow: *How can I use a prompt to bring out more creativity in students' work? What evidence of mathematical problem solving is in the students' work?*

CONCLUSION

This chapter has reviewed many strategies and tools that mentors use to work with beginning or other new teachers, including information about when to use the strategies and recommended procedures. Chapter 9 looks at common problems faced by mentors and suggests strategies for overcoming them. It then discusses the rewards of serving as a teacher-mentor.

9

Overcoming Obstacles and Reaping the Rewards

I love working with new teachers. I love working with enthusiastic and dedicated people. I learn from them and try to make them see that teaching is a learning process. I feel that, as a mentor, I am helping new teachers adjust to the rigorous life of a teacher, yet understand their importance in a child's life. I'm preparing them so that I can retire feeling that I'm leaving our schools in safe hands. Working with new teachers makes me have faith in the future of public education—most of them are great teachers!

—A mentor (Jonson, 1999b)

If teachers in general are dedicated educators, mentors are optimally so. Not only are they competent teachers, but they are teachers who willingly extend themselves, continually helping others while seeking professional growth and personal rejuvenation.

A now-classic synthesis of the research on mentoring beginning teachers (Gray & Gray, 1985) revealed that exemplary mentors

- are secure,
- have power and expertise,

- are goal oriented,
- like and trust their mentees,
- take a personal interest in the careers of their mentees,
- encourage their mentees for their ideas, and
- help their mentees gain confidence and become self-directed professionals.

Many who have taken on the challenge agree that the decision to accept a mentorship role can lead to one of the most professionally rewarding experiences of a teacher's career. No matter how competent the individual teacher and how great the motivation, however, mentoring is ultimately a lot of work, requiring both time and commitment beyond the already significant time and commitment required of a teacher. If the mentor becomes caught up in one or more of several potential pitfalls associated with the position, the decision to serve as a mentor can lead to considerable frustration.

What are some of these potential pitfalls? How can a successful mentor overcome the obstacles? And why would a teacher take the position anyway? The pitfalls can be serious, but those who avoid them will find plenty of payoffs.

THE PITFALLS

Unless a protégé is explicit in the discussion of her learning, a mentor cannot always be sure what new ideas are being assimilated. I may come to the end of a mentoring relationship and be unclear about what has been accomplished. But I have learned that some ideas will not be absorbed until a future time. I may need to be satisfied with little things, such as a comment, a smile, a willingness to learn. (Fraser, 1998, p. 51)

There are times when mentors may not be sure of what they are accomplishing or whether their long hours and exhausting efforts are bearing results. This is certainly one of the intangible, sometimes frustrating, aspects of the responsibility, which counters the many times when mentors can clearly see the results of their input. It is only one of many potential pitfalls, however. Behaviors associated with other pitfalls—some of which can be guarded against—fall into roughly four categories:

1. Overextending

2. Proceeding without clarification of the mentor's role
   a. From the administration
   b. From the mentee

3. Assuming too much responsibility for the mentee
   a. Who is less than qualified
   b. Who is unwilling

4. Underutilizing professional growth opportunities

FINDING TIME

To avoid the pitfall of overextending themselves, teachers need to be effective managers of their personal and professional lives—and, importantly, of their time. A survey in Marin County, California asked five mentors for new teachers about their experiences and insights regarding effective mentoring (Smith, 1993, p. 10). All five were glad to be mentors (p. 16), they said, but they discussed "nonsuccesses" in their efforts as well as "successes." All of these mentors felt that they were spread too thin, that they didn't have enough time to do all they wanted to do, and that funds for accomplishing their goals were limited (p. 13).

Finding time can be a challenge for any mentor. Some programs are set up to help alleviate this problem; they release mentors from some or all of their other teaching responsibilities or hire retired teachers to serve as mentors. But in many programs, teachers are expected to combine their responsibilities as a mentor with their full-time teaching responsibilities. In these cases especially, the mentor needs to manage time well. Discussing time issues up front with the mentee and as needed throughout the relationship can help both parties keep perspective and focus on learning goals. Some of the following strategies might help:

- Begin the relationship with a frank discussion about time, the need to focus and use time well, and the need to come to meetings prepared so as not to waste time.
- For informal discussions, combine goals. For example, help mentees set up their rooms while also discussing their objectives for the year.
- Hold informal discussions over lunch, while on bus or cafeteria duty, or between sessions at school- or district-wide meetings.
- For formal discussions, schedule time in advance. Begin each discussion with a review or update of relevant information to regain focus, and then keep the focus throughout the discussion.
- For observations, obtain a videotape of a mentee conducting a lesson to be discussed at a convenient time.
- Use e-mail, fax, and telephone to answer brief questions. Be sure to set limits. For example, let mentees know when they may call and how soon they can expect a response to e-mail questions.
- Have the mentee keep a journal that can be reviewed for response at the mentor's convenience.

- Seek administrative assistance in scheduling common prep times or getting the help of a substitute for release time. Another teacher might be asked to cover the mentor's class during a prep period so that the mentor can observe the mentee, for example.
- With the permission of site administration, combine two classes for an activity or lesson; the mentor may then demonstrate a skill or observe the mentee in action.
- Form teams (Heller, 2004, p. 83). Have one teacher use a prep period to take another's class, for example, thus relieving the second teacher to observe a mentee.
- Dedicate paraprofessionals to the program (Heller, 2004, p. 83). These paraprofessionals could free teachers for observations, conferences, and other tasks.
- If progress seems slow, consider taking a time-out. A pause may give the mentee a chance to absorb new information and reflect on learning.
- Set priorities; avoid committing to many other activities simultaneously.

This last point is particularly important. Many teachers have "caretaker personalities": they care for and give to others much more than they take care of themselves. Because of their professional commitment, teachers all too often find themselves saying "yes." They might join a text adoption committee, participate in curriculum planning, supervise a student group, and—serve as a mentor. Unfortunately, some believe in the myth of a Super Teacher, a teacher who can do all that is asked—and do it perfectly. Mentors need not try to be superhuman; they need simply to strive and to care. To be available for the mentee, they must learn to choose a limited number of activities carefully and then simply say a professional "no" to other extra duties or committees. Teachers need to set realistic goals and standards and to focus on celebrating successes. They must learn to replenish and to receive in balance with their giving.

DEFINING THE ROLE

Also important for teacher-mentors is defining their role, clarifying just what they are expected to do. Of the five Marin County mentors surveyed, three expressed "a sense of confusion and anxiety because they were unclear what their jobs were and who they were accountable to" (Smith, 1993, p. 13). Mentors need to establish guidelines both with the administration and with the mentees themselves. Clarification of the role can come through training, through working with a mentor coordinator, and through ongoing communication.

Support From the Administration. Potential mentors should investigate school and district commitment to the program in terms of policy and procedure statements, budgetary allocations, and processes necessary to ensure the ongoing success of the project. Establishing clearly defined expectations between mentors and administrators is absolutely necessary. Consistent feedback and communication between these groups are also necessary, as is follow-up support.

"Remember to inform your principal of your plans," one experienced mentor advises (Jonson, 1999b). "List some ideas, activities, and other pertinent information you need to share with your principal." Supportive resources—such as additional planning time, materials, and technical assistance—do not magically appear at the onset of a mentor-teacher program. These types of continuing support, all too often absent, however, are crucial. "While training usually occurs before mentors take up their new responsibilities," writes Feiman-Nemser (1996), "mentors are more likely to develop their practice as mentors if they also have opportunities to discuss questions and problems that arise in the course of the work with novices" (p. 3).

Marin County mentors also expressed wariness about administrators who attempted to "make gray [the] line" between mentoring and evaluating; all agreed that they should not evaluate their mentees despite their administrators' wishes (Smith, 1993, pp. 13–14). In addition, all five of these mentors noted that other faculty members sometimes had negative feelings toward mentors. "I know there's all these hard feelings [that I got the job and others didn't]," one said. Mentor support groups might help combat this problem, one suggested.

Guidance From the Mentee. A beginning teacher may not clearly understand what to expect from the mentor. Is the mentor an arm of the administration? Will the mentor make unreasonable demands on the mentee's time? Can the mentor be trusted with professional concerns? Again, it is best to keep mentoring entirely separate from the teacher evaluation process and to reinforce this issue consistently with the beginning teacher.

In the Marin County survey, some of the mentors discussed nonsuccesses that were directly related to the mentees themselves. Mentors felt frustrated that the mentees were not always willing to take advantage of what was offered to them. One mentor called a meeting of new teachers in her district and was dismayed when only four came. "People said, well, I got your letter and I didn't have time to open it and it's still in my pile. . . . Or, I was going to come but I had to do this instead," the mentor reported (quoted in Smith, 1993, p. 12). All five of the mentors recognized that the new teachers were simply overwhelmed by their jobs (p. 12). One mentor also pointed out that mentees sometimes worried that others would see them as incompetent if they asked for help from a mentor (p. 13).

The mentor and the beginning teacher, then, must work together to establish the parameters of the mentor's responsibilities and expectations. One way to do this is by setting up an action plan (see Appendix B). Working together on such a plan allows both parties to address their needs and concerns and helps them feel comfortable within their respective roles.

WORKING WITH DIFFICULT MENTEES

When mentors become overly involved with the beginning teacher, they may assume too much responsibility for the mentee and foster a relationship of dependency. The mentor may be overprotective or assume too many obligations to ensure the mentee's success. Some mentees are simply difficult to work with, and it is important in these cases that mentors have a clearly defined concept of facilitating as compared to defending. Mentors may also face the unwelcome reality that a beginning teacher has significant deficiencies or problems beyond the mentor's ability or authority to address.

Occasionally a mentor may feel an ethical obligation to report problems when mentees' actions are harmful to students in their care. The best approach in such a situation will depend on existing school policies and procedures. A decision to break confidentiality and seek assistance should not be viewed as failure on the part of the mentor, but more as a professional responsibility—one to be handled prudently and with sensitivity.

The Less-Than-Qualified Mentee. A mentor may on occasion work with a teacher who simply isn't qualified to be a good teacher. In some cases, the teacher has received an emergency credential without completing the usual course of study. There is an acute shortage of qualified mathematics and science teachers, for example, especially in low-income and high-minority schools, and this leads to the hiring of individuals who are not fully qualified. Some districts still view teachers as an expense and not as an asset and prefer to hire untrained teachers who cost less than qualified teachers with more education and experience. In other cases, a teacher has completed appropriate training but just doesn't understand how to work with children. In some of these situations, the mentor may need to accept that a mentee simply doesn't have the knowledge and skills necessary to become a qualified teacher.

Investing in teachers' professional knowledge and development can pay off, not only in the classroom but in the profession as a whole. But occasionally mentees who perform poorly may need be removed from their positions. This has legal ramifications, and in such situations, it is important for the mentor to turn the case over to the principal. Most principals were probably wary from the beginning about hiring an underqualified teacher, but in many cases the pool of qualified applicants was limited.

The Unwilling Mentee. At other times, a mentee may not want the assistance of a mentor or may seem to challenge the mentor at every opportunity. One teacher, Sophie, for example, often seemed not to listen to discussions, refused to stay focused, and neglected to meet deadlines for review of her work (Shulman & Sato, 2006, pp. 171–185). The mentor working with this new teacher wondered if she should continue to try to help the teacher or if it would be better for the teacher to become discouraged and leave the profession. The mentor continued to help but also set boundaries; when Sophie asked for assistance after a deadline had passed, the mentor refused to give it.

In dealing with a difficult mentee such as Sophie, it is important to be specific about expectations concerning the relationship. The mentor should make clear that information shared will be confidential, thus encouraging open discussion. Expectations for participation in discussions should also be explained clearly. For example, mentors might tell the new teacher that they will stop a discussion that becomes heated and revisit the issue later if it seems appropriate.

In a discussion about how to lead workshops, Portner gives tips for dealing with difficult questions. Several of his suggestions apply to mentor-mentee situations as well (2006, p. 45). He suggests the following:

- Anticipate awkward questions. Think about good ways to answer them before being put on the spot.
- Listen carefully when the mentee asks questions. Take care to hear the entire question before responding.
- Be willing to admit that you don't know the answer to a question.
- Avoid doing all of the talking. Continue attempting to get the mentee to participate actively.

UNDERUTILIZING PROFESSIONAL GROWTH OPPORTUNITIES

One major misconception is that teaching is relatively simple and easy to learn. In the psychological and developmental literature, however, it is widely recognized that novices do not learn simply by copying or modeling what experts do. Instead, professional growth in teaching has an emerging quality and takes a substantial amount of time. Furthermore, complex understandings and skills follow developmental patterns similar to those of other complex learning endeavors.

To assist beginning teachers in their route from novice to expert, the mentor must not only understand these precepts but also be able to facilitate the beginner's professional growth through a variety of methods and techniques. Mentors must incorporate into their professional repertoire various skills, including working with adult learners, conducting observations and data collections, problem solving, demonstrating empathy, and providing constructive criticism. It is incumbent that mentors take advantage of professional growth opportunities not only to enrich themselves but also to better enable their mentees' growth.

Any effective mentoring program incorporates training components for both mentors and beginning teachers. Unfortunately, because of poor communications and lack of program support or for various other reasons, teachers participating in district-sponsored mentoring programs sometimes find that obtaining release for training is confusing and difficult at best. Essential opportunities and resources are not always available. Again, mentors need to communicate with administrators and clarify specific details and procedures for the program before assuming the mentor role.

> Take care not to let your added responsibilities eclipse your own personal and professional growth and development. You can't give what you don't have.
>
> —A mentor's advice

THE PAYOFFS

> I like helping people. I like being validated for my skill and being paid as a professional. I get to see what other teachers are doing, and I use their ideas as well. Those teachers also serve as a resource for future mentees who might benefit from their expertise.
>
> —A mentor (Jonson, 1999b)

So why *do* teachers agree to be mentors? They do so because the payoffs are many and generally, for dedicated mentors, exceed the pitfalls. These payoffs include, but are not limited to, the satisfaction of helping strengthen the profession, the enrichment that comes with professional sharing, the satisfaction of helping the novice grow, the possibility of receiving cutting-edge training in relation to the position, visibility within the educational community, an expanded career role, personal rejuvenation, heightened prestige, and basic appreciation from the mentee (see Figure 9.1). Credit for advancement on the salary schedule and release time from other responsibilities are two other potential payoffs.

Lortie (1975) classifies possible incentives and rewards for educators into three groups: extrinsic, ancillary, and intrinsic. *Extrinsic* rewards include things that come from the outside—things such as money and prestige. *Ancillary* rewards remain constant and are considered part of the job—in teaching, these might include unpaid summer vacations, professional conferences, and tenure. *Intrinsic* rewards, such as recognition and self-satisfaction, are more personal (internal) and vary among people (Orlich, 1989, p. 72). Among mentors, intrinsic rewards play a large role as incentives, with extrinsic rewards also playing a part.

As a less tangible reward, mentors are likely to improve their own teaching in the process of helping the mentee improve. In fact, Moran (1990) suggests, "It may even be true that the greater professional development

Figure 9.1   The payoffs

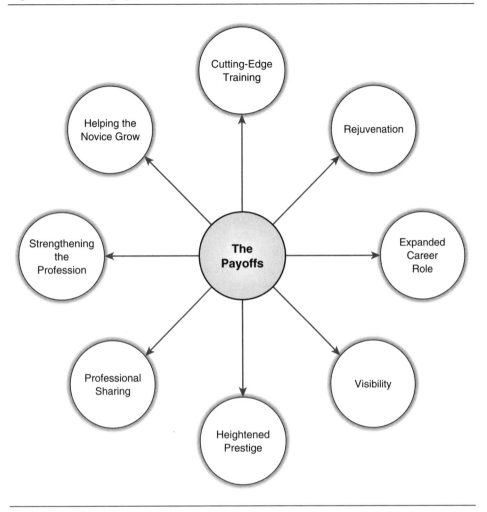

accrues to the experienced teacher, who benefits from giving voice to phi-losophy and practice" (p. 212). Mentors are likely through their work to become more aware of their own development as teachers and of the ratio-nale for their teaching strategies. They may come to appreciate the diverse styles of other teachers as well (Smith, 1993, p. 9). A mentee may even demonstrate a particular technique new to the mentor.

Affecting the practice of experienced educators is an important benefit of new teacher-mentoring programs. Mentors who have participated in training programs on standards-based professional development share a common language in discussing what constitutes effective teacher prac-tice. A survey of Connecticut special educators who were trained as men-tors and portfolio scorers showed that 83% of participants made at least moderate changes in their own classroom practices as a result of the training.

One teacher in Connecticut's BEST Program commented, "Going through the portfolio process has reminded me to include conscious reflection on lessons to target what worked and what needs to change" (Alliance for Excellent Educators, 2004).

In Tangipahoa Parish, Louisiana, mentors praised the new teacher induction program as a way to improve their own teaching skills. One mentor explained, "Being a mentor has kept me in touch with what's new in the field and has kept me fresh and motivated. I have been able to help the teachers that I work with, but they have also benefited me." Sentiments like these were echoed throughout teacher evaluations of the Tangipahoa FIRST program.

Another indirect payoff is increased professionalism. In Toledo, Ohio, the new teacher induction program has formed teachers into a community of learners over the years. According to Dal Lawrence of the Toledo Federation of Teachers, "The Toledo Plan began to change the way in which teachers think about their practice and each other's practice, as well as their accountability and responsibility for overall competence and excellence. We didn't see that happening when we started out, but it definitely exists now." Creating a culture of educators who take responsibility for themselves and their colleagues is no small feat. Participation in a culture such as this makes it possible for teachers to grow and thrive.

In a study of 158 mentors of student teachers from the University of California, Irvine, beginning in 1991, mentors filled out questionnaires regarding the benefits they saw from working with mentees (Clinard & Ariav, 1998). Although the mentees in this study were student teachers, the issues explored are relevant to any mentor working with a beginning teacher. Researchers were interested in learning the following:

1. What benefits do mentors gain from working with student teachers?

2. Is the mentoring experience having any effect on the mentors' practice (with their students)?

3. Is the mentoring experience having any effect on the mentors beyond the classroom (as professionals and as private individuals)?

Participants ranked benefits in each of these three categories after working with their mentees. See Tables 9.1 through 9.3 for their responses.

Ultimately, as Bruce Joyce and Beverly Showers (1995) suggest, a powerful incentive for any staff development activity is simply "the clear understanding that it produces success" (Orlich, 1989, p. 74). And although collegial relationships among teachers are valuable in general, the results of mentor-mentee projects are particularly impressive. See Box 9.1 for mentors' comments about their experiences.

Table 9.1   Benefits Gained From Working With Student Teachers

	UCI Mentors	
Benefits	Average[a]	Rank
Enthusiasm	3.50	1
Opportunity to collaborate	3.34	2
Knowledge of subject matter	2.93	3
Reflective mirror	2.90	4
Innovative strategies for teaching	2.90	4
Technology expertise	2.76	5
Insights about individual students' background	2.54	6
Assessment strategies	2.34	7
Sheltered language insights	1.68	8
Bilingual skills and strategies	1.20	9
Working with mainstreamed students	—	—

SOURCE: Clinard & Ariav (1998, p. 10, table 1). What mentoring does for mentors: A cross-cultural perspective. *European Journal of Teacher Education, 21*(1), 91–108.

a. Scale in questionnaire was from 0 ("very little contribution") to 4 ("great contribution"). N:89 (out of 158 participating mentors).

Table 9.2   Impact of Coaching Experience on Mentors' Work in Their Own Classrooms

	UCI Mentors	
Practice Areas	Average[a]	Rank
Reflecting more often on planning and implementation	3.02	1
Using cognitive coaching techniques with students in the classroom	2.56	2
Reassessing classroom management and discipline strategies	2.56	2
Using instructional technology more frequently and effectively	2.44	3
Collaborating more with other teachers	2.27	4

SOURCE: Clinard & Ariav (1998, p. 13, table 2). What mentoring does for mentors: A cross-cultural perspective. *European Journal of Teacher Education, 21*(1), 91–108.

a. Scale in questionnaire was from 0 ("very little contribution") to 4 ("great contribution"). N:89 (out of 158 participating mentors).

Table 9.3   Impact of the Coaching Experience Beyond the Classroom

	Average[a]	Rank
Professional Life		
More committed to quality teacher education	3.26	1
Validation as a colleague working with university/college	3.07	2
Renewed enjoyment of/enthusiasm about teaching	3.06	2
Increased respect for university/college faculty	2.89	3
More motivated to invest in the profession	2.37	4
Considering teacher education as a future career	1.89	5
Private Life		
Experienced sense of pride as an individual	2.90	1
More effectively helping people do their own thinking/problem solving	2.80	2
Demonstrating more respect in relationships	2.52	3
Communicating/interacting with others more confidently	2.50	4
Changed attitudes in dealing with family members	1.22	5

SOURCE: Clinard & Ariav (1998, p. 16, table 3). What mentoring does for mentors: A cross-cultural perspective. *European Journal of Teacher Education, 21*(1), 91–108.

a. Scale in questionnaire was from 0 ("very little contribution") to 4 ("great contribution"). N:89 (out of 158 participating mentors).

BOX 9.1

From the Mentor's Mouth

The following quotations are from teachers experienced with mentoring programs. As these teachers indicate, mentors gain as much or more from their participation as do the beginning teachers.

When teachers share their unique talents, there is a sense of electricity in the air. The Mentor Program provides an environment for this excitement to occur. It brings teachers together to share and grow professionally.

I consider it a privilege to work with my colleagues in an exciting, innovative program for teachers.

Teachers learn from students and from each other. I find mentor work stimulating, and it keeps teaching interesting. The stipend for conferences and educational materials keeps me on top of the latest methods, trends, and ideas in teaching.

More than anything, I want to see teachers stay in the profession so they, too, can enjoy the same benefits without the feeling of being lost, or alone, as I did starting out.

The exchange of ideas helps my teaching. Intellectual discussions with a colleague are stimulating. In helping mentees, I learn more, stay more current. Also, I enjoy the status.

I enjoy working with teachers—they're like your best students—but even more dedicated and appreciative.

I learn new techniques. It's very beneficial being paired with a recently trained teacher.

I was a new teacher and received tremendous support even though I was very overwhelmed. I truly believe that a support system can help teachers succeed and deal with all the demands of being a new teacher. . . . Collaboration keeps me engaged, interested, and motivated, and I hope to provide that for others.

I am interested in seeing the curriculum that I've developed over the past 25 years continue as a legacy to that mentee and future generations of her students.

I find it very rewarding to work with other teachers [with various levels of experience]. Also, I am dedicated to education, and mentoring offers a unique opportunity to help new teachers.

I get reenergized by working with beginning teachers. I get new ideas and try out new approaches.

SOURCE: Jonson (1999b).

CONCLUSION

When teachers have the autonomy, opportunity, time, and resources to participate in their own and their colleagues' professional growth, instructional improvement is the obvious consequence. The collegial nature of the mentoring relationship, and of the larger mentoring program, means that all involved contribute to its growth and reap its benefits.

Being concerned for others is an important stage in career development. At the utilitarian level, mentors help their own careers by helping others. At the altruistic level, one mentor expressed the feeling well in saying, "I sleep better at night because I do for others what I wish had been done for me!" Another mentor explains,

> Being a mentor keeps me current. When I have to answer my mentee's questions, it makes me ask, "Why am I doing what I'm doing?" In discussing philosophy, problems, or techniques with this new teacher, I find out what I really believe. That makes me a stronger person and a better teacher (Gordon & Maxey, 2000, p. 34).

PART III

Putting It All Together

Come to the edge, he said. They said: We are afraid. Come to the edge, he said. They came. He pushed them . . . and they flew.

—Guillaume Apollinaire

There is little doubt that ongoing, meaningful contact between mentors and new teachers reinforces and fosters professional development. The following pages contain a month-by-month calendar of activities designed to promote interaction between these teachers. Activities are selected for each month to correspond with typical events occurring during a school year. Note that this calendar is set up on a traditional schedule, with teachers starting their work of planning in August and beginning in the classroom in September. Adjustments may need to be made for districts where the schedule is year-round or differs in some other way from that presented here.

Activities and topics were selected by reviewing research on the needs of beginning teachers and the experiences reported by mentors and mentees. Mentors and mentees are encouraged to review these activities as a team, to modify them as needed, and to create other activities of their own to maximize the development of their relationship. Activities for school, district, and university involvement, depending on the purposes and extent of the program, are also included. A review of the calendar several months in advance to anticipate needs and plan activities might be useful. Be sure to check the local school, district, and state for requirements and deadlines that need to be incorporated as well. Conference times in individual schools may vary, for example, or statewide testing schedules may need to be incorporated. Jot down any ideas in the process of working through this calendar; room has been left for making notes.

Following the month-by-month calendar is a year-at-a-glance check-list. This is a condensed version of the calendar, listing major activities to be checked off. By working together on these activities and others of their own choice, the mentor and mentee will build the trusting relationship that will lead to meaningful teacher development for both.

MONTH-BY-MONTH MENTORING ACTIVITIES

AUGUST (or one month prior to start of school)

Mentoring Activities and Ideas

___ Meet and welcome mentee.
- Welcome mentee in a telephone call before the start of school.
- Take mentee on tour of school building.
- Introduce mentee to other teachers and staff.

___ Work on developing collegial relationship.
- Have coffee or lunch away from building.
- Attend social gatherings together or meet in some social setting.

___ Help mentee set up room.

___ Communicate with principal.
- Send informal note about making contact with mentee and about initial plans.

School/District/University Activities

___ Match mentors and mentees.

___ Notify mentor-mentee teams of matches.

___ Hold orientation or social gathering.

___ Schedule workshops.

Things to Keep in Mind

- Remember: Early contact is essential.
- Establish a system for ongoing communication.
- Orientation or a social gathering is important to success.

SEPTEMBER (or first month of school)

Mentoring Activities and Ideas

___ Hold informal meetings.
- "Drop in" to touch base with mentee.
- With mentee, analyze class composition (gender, ethnicity, achievement scores, friendship/rivalries).
- Share a funny or interesting event that happened during the day.
- Write occasional notes acknowledging or supporting mentee's activities and successes.
- Meet informally for coffee.

___ Hold bimonthly conferences to discuss

- Keeping gradebooks
- Maintaining student discipline
- Managing classroom instruction
- Obtaining supplies
- School policies and procedures
- Homework and makeup work policies
- Maximizing academic learning time
- Preparing for parent conferences, contacting parents

___ Help mentee socialize within school.

- Discuss school norms, social traditions.
- Introduce mentee to other staff.
- Show mentee where to find supplies, materials, and so on.
- Review standard operating procedures.

___ Work on collegial relationship with mentee.

- Continue frequent communication and contact.

___ Plan mentor activities with mentee.

- Cooperatively develop flexible Mentor-Mentee Action Plan.

___ Arrange demonstration lesson for mentee.

- Schedule demonstration lesson to be observed and followed up by conference.
- Conduct initial demonstration in mentor's classroom.

___ Communicate with principal.

School/District/University Activities

___ Encourage and support activities.

___ Plan workshops for mentors, mentees, or both.

Things to Keep in Mind

- Be very accessible the first day and week of school.
- Your relationship is key to success.
- Hold at least one scheduled meeting with mentee bimonthly. Focus at meeting on specific ideas and concerns (see specific suggestions for each month).
- "Socialization" includes written and unwritten rules of "how things work around here."
- Tell the school principal about your initial contact and planning with your mentee, but not about mentee performance.
- Focus on developing a professional, collegial relationship—more than just a friendship.

- See Appendix B for Action Plan examples and forms you can use.
- Refer to "Demonstration Teaching" in Chapter 8 for procedure.
- Have fun!

OCTOBER (or second month of school)

Mentoring Activities and Ideas

___ Hold bimonthly conferences to discuss
- Parent conferencing, parent contacts
- Report cards
- Classroom management
- Discipline
- Managing instructional tasks, time management
- Audiovisual department
- Student motivation and feedback
- Mentor-Mentee Action Plan
- Mentee's goals and professional development plan

___ Observe mentee and give feedback.
- Schedule observation with pre- and postconference time.
- Identify focus for next observation.

___ Hold informal discussions.
- Continue to share events and happenings of the day.

___ Share resources for professional development opportunities, such as
- State and county offices of education and similar supporting agencies
- Local university and college courses
- District staff development programs

___ Communicate with principal.

School/District/University Activities

___ Plan activities to encourage communication and to allow mentors and mentees to share experiences.

___ Consider using principals, district office staff, state and county offices of education, and staff from other supporting agencies in planning mentor-mentee activities.

Things to Keep in Mind

- The first formal observation should be nonthreatening; refer to "Observation and Feedback" in Chapter 8.

- Consider taking a university class together with your mentee or attending a workshop together.

NOVEMBER (or third month of school)

Mentoring Activities and Ideas

___ Hold bimonthly conferences to discuss
- Parent conferences, communications
- Feedback to students
- Curriculum resources and materials
- Mentor-Mentee Action Plan
- Arrangements for substitute teachers

___ Continue observation and feedback.

___ Continue discussions about professional development opportunities.

___ Communicate with principal.

Things to Keep in Mind

- Check your district and building calendars to anticipate upcoming activities you should discuss or plan for.
- Schedule opportunities for your mentee to observe other teachers. Make suggestions and help with arrangements if appropriate.
- Recognize that this is often a difficult month for new teachers.

DECEMBER (or fourth month of school)

Mentoring Activities and Ideas

___ Hold bimonthly conferences to discuss
- School traditions
- School and district policies regarding holiday events and activities

___ Communicate informally.
- Write short notes of reinforcement and support.

___ Hold formal observation and conference.

___ Communicate with principal.

Things to Keep in Mind

- Because of holidays, you may not want to do observations this month. Talk it over with your mentee.

JANUARY (or fifth month of school)

Mentoring Activities and Ideas

___ Hold bimonthly conferences to discuss
- School and classroom procedures for ending and beginning the semester
- Report cards and grading
- Curriculum resources
- Promoting positive relationships among students and teachers
- Student work/progress thus far
- Mentor-Mentee Action Plan

___ Review first-term experiences.
- Discuss highlights.
- Evaluate growth experiences.
- Celebrate successes.

___ Celebrate completion of first term.
- Plan visible recognition.

___ Continue informal communications.

___ Communicate with principal.

School/District/University Activities

___ Review experiences and evaluate current success of program with mentors or supervisors; identify any modifications needed.

Things to Keep in Mind

- Reflection helps promote learning and growth.
- Be creative! Involve mentee's students in celebration.
- Informal communications are still very important; look for new opportunities.
- Continue communication with principal.

FEBRUARY (or sixth month of school)

Mentoring Activities and Ideas

___ Hold bimonthly conferences to
- Plan activities for second semester
- Review and discuss district office staff roles, departments, and support services
- Share literature, research readings, and professional journals

- Review Mentor-Mentee Action Plan
- Discuss use of community resources, such as guest speakers and field trips
- Discuss standardized testing

___ Continue informal communications.

___ Communicate with principal.

Things to Keep in Mind

- A plan is very helpful, but it should be reviewed and modified regularly as needs change.
- Be sure to check with the local district and state for mandated test schedules, and build in preparation for tests.

MARCH (or seventh month of school)

Mentoring Activities and Ideas

___ Hold bimonthly conferences to discuss
- Mentee's concerns and needs
- Professional organizations
- Mentor-Mentee Action Plan

___ Arrange for mentee observation of other teachers.

___ Work on peer-based relationship with mentee.

___ Continue informal communications.

___ Discuss type of observations needed.

___ Communicate with principal.

School/District/University Activities

___ Hold inservice workshops for mentors, mentees, or both.

Things to Keep in Mind

- Your mentee may not be familiar with various professional associations and with the relative advantages of membership.
- Mentees will continue to benefit from observations of other teachers.
- Be specific when identifying needs and giving feedback.
- Be sure to make known your own inservice needs and those of other mentors.

APRIL (or eighth month of school)

Mentoring Activities and Ideas

___ Hold bimonthly conferences.
- Discuss career planning and development.
- Talk about testing and evaluation services.
- Review Mentor-Mentee Action Plan.
- Begin discussion of bringing the year to a close.

___ Continue informal communications.

___ Continue Action Plan activities.

___ Communicate with principal.

Things to Keep in Mind

- Focus on building the mentee's autonomy and self-confidence.

MAY (or ninth month of school)

Mentoring Activities and Ideas

___ Hold bimonthly conferences.
- Discuss procedures for ending the year.
- Discuss procedures for beginning the following year.

___ Revise mentor-mentee activities.

___ Continue informal communications.

___ Build and reinforce peer relationship.

___ Communicate with principal.

School/District/University Activities

___ Celebrate completion of first year of teaching with
- Awards or certificates signed by the superintendent, principal, or director of teacher education program
- Recognition banquet for mentors and mentees

Things to Keep in Mind

- Begin to move the mentor-mentee relationship away from previously established schedules and patterns.
- Continue to focus on mentee autonomy, self-confidence, and self-direction.
- Review, reflect, and celebrate!

JUNE (or final month of school)

Mentoring Activities and Ideas

___ Hold bimonthly conferences to
  - Discuss mentee concerns
  - Review year's events

___ Continue recognition of mentee and of mentoring program.

___ Communicate with principal.

School/District/University Activities

___ Evaluate program.

___ Identify goals for next year.

Things to Keep in Mind

- This is a time to reflect on the year just ending and to think of its impact on the year to come.
- The benefits of the program should remain visible to the staff.
- This is a great time to hold a meeting of all mentors.

YEAR-AT-A-GLANCE CHECKLIST

AUGUST (or one month prior to start of school)

___ Meet and welcome mentee.

___ Work on developing collegial relationship.

___ Help mentee set up room.

___ Communicate with principal.

___ Begin participation in school/district/university activities.

SEPTEMBER (or first month of school)

___ Hold informal meetings.

___ Hold bimonthly conferences.

___ Help mentee socialize within school.

___ Work on collegial relationship with mentee.

___ Plan mentor activities with mentee.

___ Arrange demonstration lesson for mentee.

___ Communicate with principal.

OCTOBER (or second month of school)

___ Hold bimonthly conferences.

___ Observe mentee and give feedback.

___ Hold informal discussions.

___ Share resources for professional development opportunities.

___ Communicate with principal.

NOVEMBER (or third month of school)

___ Hold bimonthly conferences.

___ Continue observation and feedback.

___ Continue discussions about professional development opportunities.

___ Communicate with principal.

DECEMBER (or fourth month of school)

___ Hold bimonthly conferences.

___ Communicate informally.

___ Hold formal observation and conference.

___ Communicate with principal.

JANUARY (or fifth month of school)

___ Hold bimonthly conferences.

___ Review first-term experiences.

___ Celebrate completion of first term.

___ Continue informal communications.

___ Communicate with principal.

FEBRUARY (or sixth month of school)

___ Hold bimonthly conferences.

___ Continue informal communications.

___ Communicate with principal.

MARCH (or seventh month of school)

___ Hold bimonthly conferences.

___ Arrange for mentee observation of other teachers.

___ Work on peer-based relationship with mentee.

___ Continue informal communications.

___ Discuss type of observations needed.

___ Communicate with principal.

APRIL (or eighth month of school)

___ Hold bimonthly conferences.

___ Continue informal communications.

___ Continue Action Plan activities.

___ Communicate with principal.

MAY (or ninth month of school)

___ Hold bimonthly conferences.

___ Revise mentor-mentee activities.

___ Continue informal communications.

___ Build and reinforce peer relationship.

___ Communicate with principal.

JUNE (or final month of school)

___ Hold bimonthly conferences.

___ Continue recognition of mentee and of mentoring program.

___ Communicate with principal.

___ Complete school/district/university activities.

Appendix A

FIRST-DAY CHECKLIST

The first days of school are critical for a new teacher. Harry Wong says that teachers determine their success or failure for the rest of the school year by what they do on the first days (Wong & Wong, 1991). Student achievement at the end of the year is directly related to the degree to which the teacher establishes good control of the classroom procedures in the very first week of the school year. Few beginning teachers receive any instruction on what to do on the first day of school, however, and few get any experience or training during student teaching on what to do on that day.

To prepare for the first day, the beginning teacher often needs help from a mentor. The beginning teacher needs to think through all the specific procedures needed to maintain a classroom environment in which instruction and learning can occur. The beginning teacher and mentor can discuss in advance which practices and procedures the beginning teacher will establish and how to communicate these carefully to students so they will know what to expect. The checklist provided here is offered as a discussion starter.

CHECKLIST

Preparing for the First Day

Efficiency in the classroom is the hallmark of an effective learning environment. Established procedures, taught to students at the onset of the school year and consistently applied, will significantly improve classroom management time.

Directions:

- Check each item for which you already have a prepared process.
- Place an X by each item for which you do not have a policy but believe you need one.
- Highlight those items that you will teach the students the first day of class.

I. Beginning Class

___ A. Roll call, absent, tardy

___ B. Academic warm-ups

___ C. Distributing materials

___ D. Class opening

II. Room/School Areas

___ A. Shared materials

___ B. Teacher's desk

___ C. Drinks, bathroom, pencil sharpener

___ D. Student storage/lockers

___ E. Student desks

___ F. Learning centers, stations

___ G. Playground, school grounds

___ H. Lunchroom

___ I. Halls

III. Setting Up Independent Work

___ A. Defining "working alone"

___ B. Identifying problems

___ C. Identifying resources

___ D. Identifying solutions

___ E. Scheduling

___ F. Interim checkpoints

IV. Instructional Activities

___ A. Teacher, student contacts

___ B. Student movement in the room

___ C. Signals for students' attention

___ D. Signals for teacher's attention

___ E. Student talk during seatwork

___ F. Activities to do when work is done

___ G. Student participation

___ H. Laboratory procedures

___ I. Movement in and out of small groups

___ J. Bringing materials to school

___ K. Expected behavior in group

___ L. Behavior of students not in group

V. Ending Class

___ A. Putting away supplies, equipment

___ B. Cleaning up

___ C. Organizing class materials

___ D. Dismissing class

VI. Interruptions

___ A. Rules

___ B. Talk among students

___ C. Conduct

___ D. Passing out books, supplies

___ E. Turning in work

___ F. Handing back assignments

___ G. Getting back assignments

___ H. Out-of-seat policies

___ I. Consequences for misbehavior

VII. Other Procedures

___ A. Fire drills

___ B. Lunch procedures

___ C. Student helpers

___ D. Safety procedures

VIII. Work Requirements

___ A. Heading papers

___ B. Use of pen or pencil

___ C. Writing on back of paper

___ D. Neatness, legibility

___ E. Incomplete work

___ F. Late work

___ G. Missed work

___ H. Due dates

___ I. Makeup work

___ J. Supplies

___ K. Coloring or drawing on paper

___ L. Use of manuscript or cursive

IX. Communicating Assignments

___ A. Posting assignments

___ B. Orally giving assignments

___ C. Provision for absentees

___ D. Long-term assignments

___ E. Term schedule

___ F. Homework assignments

X. Student Work

___ A. In-class participation

___ B. In-class assignments

___ C. Homework

___ D. Stages of long-term assignments

XI. Checking Assignments in Class

___ A. Students exchanging papers

___ B. Marking and grading assignments

___ C. Turning in assignments

___ D. Students correcting errors

XII. Grading Procedures

___ A. Determining grades

___ B. Recording grades

___ C. Grading long assignments

___ D. Extra-credit work

___ E. Keeping papers, grades, assignments

___ F. Grading criteria

___ G. Contracting for grades

XIII. Academic Feedback

___ A. Rewards and incentives

___ B. Posting student work

___ C. Communicating with parents

___ D. Students' record of grades

___ E. Written comments on assignments

SOURCE: Adapted from *Achieving Excellence,* Mid-Continent Regional Educational Laboratory, Kansas City, MO, 1983.

Appendix B

MENTOR-MENTEE ACTION PLANS

Mentor-Mentee Action Plans can be designed as a collaborative guide for mentors and mentees as they conjointly plan their activities for the academic year. Typically, an Action Plan serves three functions:

1. To clarify the roles and responsibilities of the mentor and mentee

2. To provide a focus and framework for mentor-mentee teamwork

3. To become an informative resource when shared with others

Several sample Mentor-Mentee Action Plans follow. Take a look to see if this sort of planning would work for you. Check with your school or district to see if it has a similar planning form.

SAMPLE ELEMENTARY LEVEL
MENTOR-MENTEE ACTION PLAN

Mentor: _____

Mentee: _____

School/District: _____

Date: _____

Three Priority Goals for the Year

I. To obtain a broad view of teaching styles and strategies

II. To develop mastery of second-grade curriculum

III. To maximize time spent on learning tasks

Objectives	Activity (what, who, where, dates)	Evidence of Completion/Successes
I. Broaden view of styles/strategies.	Do observation in multiage classrooms (Nov).	Observed at ____ Elementary School on Nov 9: strategy of guided reading groups
A. Become familiar with three new teaching strategies.	Take coursework in curriculum integration (10 clock hours Jan/Feb).	Integrated arts into curriculum
B. Attempt use of one new strategy.	Have debriefing sessions following observations.	Viewed instructional videotapes on teaching math with manipulatives (May)
	Attend workshop Jan 25.	Taught thinking skill explicitly

II. Mastery of curriculum	Locate videos, tapes, and books that support units of study.	Now know who to contact for resources and know location of many additional materials
A. Build bank of instructional strategies.	Obtain list of extended reading materials.	Implemented alternative strategy that resulted in greater time on learning task
B. Become familiar with teaching resources.		Had observations and debriefings that were specific to teaching techniques and student responses
III. Time on task	Have observer collect data and provide feedback two times in Oct and Nov.	Implemented alternative strategy that resulted in greater time on learning task
A. Improve time management.	Brainstorm different management strategies.	Observations and debriefings were specific to teaching techniques and student responses
B. Increase time on instructional/ learning tasks.	Increase mentee's self-awareness of teaching style through self-reflection, observation, feedback, and analysis of data.	Students were observed being actively engaged Increased independent learning and self-study Completed required units of study Had positive classroom environment, which resulted in less time spent on discipline and more engaged learning time

SAMPLE MIDDLE SCHOOL LEVEL
MENTOR-MENTEE ACTION PLAN

Mentor: _____

Mentee: _____

School/District: _____

Date: _____

Three Priority Goals for the Year

I. To become comfortable with the sixth-grade curriculum and find exciting and meaningful ways to present it

II. To gain a general orientation to district and school programs

III. To incorporate cooperative learning as a teaching strategy

Objectives	Activity (what, who, where, dates)	Evidence of Completion/Successes
I. Knowledge of sixth-grade curriculum	A. Weekly Tuesday morning meetings between mentor and mentee to share curriculum materials and instruction techniques	Ongoing throughout school year
	B. Mentor and mentee plan a unit to be taught together with combined classes	Evaluation of unit by mentor and mentee upon completion
II. General orientation	A. Weekly Tuesday morning meetings between mentor and mentee	Ongoing between Sept and June
III. Cooperative learning	A. Videotape two lessons using the cooperative learning teaching strategy	Mentor and mentee observe videotaped lessons together to evaluate

SAMPLE HIGH SCHOOL LEVEL
MENTOR-MENTEE ACTION PLAN

Mentor: _____

Mentee: _____

School/District: _____

Date: _____

Three Priority Goals for the Year

I. To use effective educational strategies

II. To coordinate and integrate state, district, and school curriculum standards within the Home and Family Life Program (HFL)

III. To create a plan for the future direction of the HFL Program in the high school

Objectives	Activity (what, who, where, dates)	Evidence of Completion/Successes
I. A. Become familiar with current, effective, and innovative strategies.	A. 1. Attend Mentor/New Teacher workshop Oct 19. A. 2. Attend Anti-Smoking Training Oct 16. A. 3. Watch tapes on classroom management.	A. 1. Program, notes, agenda A. 2. Training materials, agenda A. 3. Note packet
B. Implement strategies that apply to HFL program at this school.	B. 1. Try techniques and ideas. B. 2. Teach Anti-Smoking Program to ninth graders.	B. 1. List and evaluation of effectiveness B. 2. Planbook record
C. Observe other classrooms.	C. Observe other teachers within the building (at least three) and in other schools.	C. Calendar record and employee forms

(Continued)

(Continued)

II. A. Become familiar with curriculum used at this school.	A. Review and use FLASH, Family and Futures, and Here's Looking at You.	A. Planbook record
B. Gain an understanding of the high school program.	B. 1. Arrange and attend meetings with high school HFL teacher.	B. 1. Calendar record of meetings
	B. 2. Visit and observe high school HFL and other programs.	B. 2. Employee leave forms
C. Become involved in FHA at district, region, and state levels.	C. 1. Attend Regional Day and Advisers' Workshop Oct 9.	C. 1. Employee leave forms and programs
	C. 2. Observe HFL program with a well-integrated standards.	C. 2. Employee leave forms
		C. 3. Employee leave forms and programs
		Calendar record
D. Become involved in state HFL programs.	D. Attend local HFL meetings Oct 28 and Mar 23.	
III. A. Explore innovative HFL programs.	A. Visit and observe such programs (talk to state supervisor for recommendations).	A. Employee leave forms, notes
B. Become familiar with technology and new design within HFL programs.	B. Visit and observe programs with new or state-of-the-art designs—for example, the newly remodeled high school.	B. Employee leave forms, notes, and so forth

Appendix C

Supervisory Beliefs Inventory

by Carl Glickman, Association for
Supervision and Curriculum Development

The Supervisory Beliefs Inventory (Glickman, 1985) is an excellent tool for mentors to use in thinking about the challenges of interpersonal communication and their own personal orientation to supervision. Part I is a prediction section in which individuals guess how they would place themselves. Part II is a forced-choice instrument that, if answered honestly, gives a reality index of how the individual acts. Glickman points out that one orientation is not necessarily better than the others. For a complete discussion of each of the three orientations, refer to Chapters 3 through 5 in Glickman's *Supervision of Instruction: A Developmental Approach.* See Chapter 3 in this book for more on Glickman's work. Although he uses the term "supervision," much of what he has to say applies to mentoring.

THE SUPERVISORY BELIEFS INVENTORY

This inventory is designed for supervisors to assess their own beliefs about teacher supervision and professional development. The inventory assumes that supervisors believe and act according to all three of the orientations of

SOURCE: Glickman, C. D. (1985). *Supervision of instruction: A developmental approach.* Alexandria, VA: Association for Supervision and Curriculum Development. From "Developmental Supervision: Alternative Practices for Helping Teachers Improve Instruction," by Carl D. Glickman, 1981, pp. 12–15. Alexandria, VA: Association for Supervision and Curriculum Development. Copyright © 1981 ASCD. Reprinted by permission. All rights reserved.

supervision, yet one usually dominates. The inventory is designed to be self-administered and self-scored. The second part lists items for which supervisors must choose one of two options. A scoring key follows, which can be used to compare the predictions of Part I with the actual beliefs indicated by the forced-choice items of Part II.

Part I. Predictions

Instructions: Check one answer for each question.

	Percent of Time				
Questions	Nearly 100%	About 75%	About 50%	About 20%	About 0%
1. How often do you use a *directive approach* (rather than one of the other two approaches) in supervising teachers?	_____	_____	_____	_____	_____
2. How often do you use a *collaborative approach* (rather than one of the other two approaches) in supervising teachers?	_____	_____	_____	_____	_____
3. How often do you use a *nondirective approach* (rather than one of the other two approaches) in supervising teachers?	_____	_____	_____	_____	_____

Part II. Forced Choices

Instructions: Circle either A or B for each item. You may not completely agree with either choice, but choose the one that is closest to how you feel.

1. A. Supervisors should give teachers a large degree of autonomy and initiative within broadly defined limits.

   B. Supervisors should give teachers directions about methods that will help them improve their teaching.

2. A. It is important for teachers to set their own goals and objectives for professional growth.

B. It is important for supervisors to help teachers reconcile their personalities and teaching styles with the philosophy and direction of the school.

3. A. Teachers are likely to feel uncomfortable and anxious if the objectives on which they will be evaluated are not clearly defined by the supervisor.

B. Evaluations of teachers are meaningless if teachers are not able to define with their supervisors the objectives for evaluation.

4. A. An open, trusting, warm, and personal relationship with teachers is the most important ingredient in supervising teachers.

B. A supervisor who is too intimate with teachers risks being less effective and less respected than a supervisor who keeps a certain degree of professional distance from teachers.

5. A. My role during supervisory conferences is to make the interaction positive, to share realistic information, and to help teachers plan their own solutions to problems.

B. The methods and strategies I use with teachers in a conference are aimed at our reaching agreement over the needs for future improvement.

6. In the initial phase of working with a teacher:

A. I develop objectives with each teacher that will help accomplish school goals.

B. I try to identify the talents and goals of individual teachers so they can work on their own improvement.

7. When several teachers have a similar classroom problem, I prefer to:

A. Have the teachers form an ad hoc group and help them work together to solve the problem.

B. Help teachers on an individual basis find their strengths, abilities, and resources so that each one finds his or her own solution to the problem.

8. The most important clue that an inservice workshop is needed is when:

A. The supervisor perceived that several teachers lack knowledge of skill in a specific area, which is resulting in low morale, undue stress, and less effective teaching.

B. Several teachers perceive the need to strengthen their abilities in the same instructional area.

9. A. The supervisory staff should decide the objectives of an inservice workshop since they have a broad perspective of the teachers' abilities and the school's needs.

B. Teachers and the supervisory staff should reach consensus about the objectives of an inservice workshop before the workshop is held.

10. A. Teachers who feel they are growing personally will be more effective in the classroom than teachers who are not experiencing personal growth.

B. The knowledge and ability of teaching strategies and methods that have been proven over the years should be taught and practiced by all teachers to be effective in their classrooms.

11. When I perceive that a teacher might be scolding a student unnecessarily:

A. I explain, during a conference with the teacher, why the scolding was excessive.

B. I ask the teacher about the incident but do not interject my judgment.

12. A. One effective way to improve teacher performance is to formulate clear behavioral objectives and create meaningful incentives for achieving them.

B. Behavioral objectives are rewarding and helpful to some teachers but stifling to others; also, some teachers benefit from behavioral objectives in some situations but not in others.

13. During a preobservation conference:

A. I suggest to the teacher what I could observe, but I let the teacher make the final decision about the objectives and methods of observation.

B. The teacher and I mutually decide the objectives and methods of observation.

14. A. Improvement occurs very slowly if teachers are left on their own, but when a group of teachers works together on a specific problem, they learn rapidly and their morale remains high.

B. Group activities may be enjoyable, but I find that individual, open discussion with a teacher about a problem and its possible solutions leads to more sustained results.

15. When an inservice or professional development workshop is scheduled:

A. All teachers who participated in the decision to hold the workshop should be expected to attend it.

B. Teachers, regardless of their role in forming a workshop, should be able to decide if the workshop is relevant to their personal or professional growth and, if not, should not be expected to attend.

Scoring Key

Step 1. Circle your answer from Part II of the inventory in the columns below.

Column I	Column II	Column III
1B	1A	
	2B	2A
3A	3B	
4B		4A
	5B	5A
6A		6B
	7A	7B
8A		8B
9A	9B	
10B		10A
11A		11B
12A 12B		
	13B	13A
14B 14A		
	15A	15B

Step 2. Tally the total number of circled items in each column and multiply by 6.7.

2.1 Total response in Column I _____ × 6.7 = _____

2.2 Total response in Column II _____ × 6.7 = _____

2.3 Total response in Column III _____ × 6.7 = _____

Step 3. Interpretation

The product you obtained in Step 2.1 is an approximate percentage of how often you take a directive approach to supervision, rather than either of the other two approaches. The product you obtained in Step 2.2 is an approximate percentage of how often you take a collaborative approach to supervision, rather than either of the other two approaches, and the product you obtained in Step 2.3 is an approximate percentage of how often you take a nondirective approach. The approach on which you spend the greatest percentage of time is the supervisory model that dominates your beliefs. If the percentage values are equal or close to equal, you take an eclectic approach.

You can also compare these results with your predictions in Part I.

What to Do With Your Score

You now have a base to look at the orientation with which you are most comfortable. If your scores for two or three orientations were about equal (30% nondirective, 40% collaborative, and 30% directive), you are either confused or more positively eclectic. If you are eclectic, you probably consider varying your supervisory orientations according to each situation. Practitioners of one orientation might be more effective by learning the very precise supervisory behaviors that are needed to make that orientation work. To think that supervision is collaborative is incomplete until one knows how to employ techniques that result in collaboration. Many supervisors and mentors profess to be of a certain orientation but unknowingly use behaviors that result in different outcomes.

References

Acheson, J., & Gall, M. (1980). *Techniques in the clinical supervision of teachers.* New York: Longman.

Albert, S., Blondino, C., & McGrath, J. (1990). *Peer coaching.* Seattle, WA: Puget Sound Educational Service District.

Alliance for Excellent Education. (2004, June 23). Tapping into potential: Retaining and developing high-quality new teachers. Washington DC: Author.

Association for Supervision and Curriculum Development. (1999a). *Mentoring to improve schools: Facilitator's guide.* Alexandria, VA: ASCD.

Association for Supervision and Curriculum Development. (1999b). *Mentoring to improve schools: Successful mentoring programs* [Videotape]. Alexandria, VA: ASCD.

Bacon, D. (1997, October 6). Veteran teachers lend a hand: Peer Assistance and Review Program celebrates ten years. *California Teacher, 1,* 6–7.

Bartell, C. (1995). Shaping teacher induction policy in California. *Teacher Education Quarterly, 22*(4), 27–43.

Bey, T. M. (1992). Mentoring in teacher education: Diversifying support for teachers. In T. M. Bey & C. T. Holmes (Eds.), *Mentoring: Contemporary principles and issues* (pp. 111–120). Reston, VA: Association of Teacher Educators.

Blythe, T., Allen, D., & Powell, B. S. (1999). *Looking together at student work: A companion guide to assessing student learning.* New York Teachers College Press.

Bolton, E. (1980). A conceptual analysis of the mentor relationship in the career development of women. *Adult Education, 30,* 195–297.

Bova, B. (1987). Mentoring as a learning experience. In V. J. Marsick (Ed.), *Learning in the workplace.* London: Croom Helm.

Bova, B. M., & Phillips, R. R. (1983). Mentoring as a learning experience for adults. *Journal of Teacher Education, 35*(3), 16–20.

Brennan, S., Thames, W., & Roberts, R. (1999). In Kentucky: Mentoring with a mission. *Educational Leadership, 56*(8), 49–52.

Brookfield, S. D. (1986). *Understanding and facilitating adult learning.* San Francisco: Jossey-Bass.

Brown, M. H., & Williams, A. (1977). Lifeboat ethics and the first year teacher. *Clearinghouse, 51,* 73.

Bullough, R. V. (1990). Supervision, mentoring, and self-discovery: A case study of a first year teacher. *Journal of Curriculum and Supervision, 5,* 338–360.

Bush, L. (2001). Ready to read, ready to learn: An education initiative. Retrieved January 8, 2007, from www.whitehouse.gov/firstlady/initiatives/readytore adoverview.pdf

Bush, R. N. (1996). The formative years. In *The real world of beginning teachers* (pp. 1–14). Washington, DC: National Education Foundation.

California Department of Education. (2006, February). Developing highly qualified teachers and administrators initiative. California Department of Education.

Christenbury, L. (1995). Breaking the silence. *A Word to the Wise, 1*(2), 3.

Clinard, L. M., & Ariav, T. (1998, Spring). What mentoring does for mentors: A cross-cultural perspective. *European Journal of Teacher Education, 21*(1), 91–108.

Cohen, N. H. (1995). *Mentoring adult learners: A guide for educators and trainers.* Malabar, FL: Krieger.

Commission on Teacher Credentialing. (1991). "I was really nervous, but I learned a lot": New developments in the CNTP assessment component. *Teacher News, 3*(2), 1–7.

Costa, A. L., & Garmston, R. J. (1994). *Cognitive coaching: A foundation for renaissance schools.* Norwood, MA: Christopher-Gordon.

Costa, A. L., & Kallick, B. (2000). Getting into the habit of reflection. *Educational Leadership, 57*(7), 60–62.

Daloz, L. A. (1999). *Mentor: Guiding the journey of adult learners.* San Francisco: Jossey-Bass.

Darling-Hammond, L. (1988). The futures of teaching. *Educational Leadership, 46*(3), 4–10.

Darling-Hammond, L. (2001). *The research and rhetoric on teacher certification: A response to "teacher certification reconsidered."* New York: National Commission on Teaching and America's Future.

Darling-Hammond, L. (2003). Keeping good teachers: Why it matters, what leaders can do. *Educational Leadership, 60*(8), 6–13.

Developmental Studies Center. (1998). *The master teacher handbook.* Unpublished manuscript.

Doyle, W. (1990). Classroom knowledge as a foundation for teaching. *Teachers College Record, 91*, 347–360.

Duncan, B. A. (2005, Fall). Using technology to support instructional mentoring. *Reflections, 8*(1), 8–9.

Farkas, S., Johnson, J., & Foleno, T. (2000). *A sense of calling: Who teaches and why.* New York: Public Agenda.

Feiman-Nemser, S. (1996). Teacher mentoring: A critical review. *Peer Resources.* Retrieved November 30, 2001, from www.islandnet.com/~rcarr/teachermen tors.html

Fraser, J. (1998). *Teacher to teacher: A guidebook for effective mentoring.* Portsmouth, NH: Heinemann.

Galvez-Martin, M. E., Bowman, C., & Morrison, M. (1999). ATE Newsletter, 32(6), 4.

Gandal, M., & Vranek, J. (2001). Standards: Here today, here tomorrow. *Educational Leadership, 59*(31), 6–13.

Glatthorn, A. A. (1984). *Differential supervision.* Alexandria, VA: Association for Supervision and Curriculum Development.

Glenn, W. J. (2006). Model versus mentor: Defining the necessary qualities of the effective cooperating teacher. *Teacher Education Quarterly, 33*(1), 85–95.

Gless, J., & Moir, E. Supporting beginning teachers with heart and mind: A decade of lessons learned from the Santa Cruz New Teacher Project. Retrieved September 21, 2006, from www.newteachercenter.org/article7.php.

Glickman, C. D. (2002). *Leadership for learning: How to help teachers succeed.* Alexandria, VA: Association for Supervision and Curriculum Development.

Glickman, C. D. (1985). *Supervision of instruction: A developmental approach.* Alexandria, VA: Association for Supervision and Curriculum Development.

Goodlad, J. I. (1984). *A place called school: Prospects for the future.* New York: McGraw-Hill.

Gordon, S. P., & Maxey, S. (2000). *How to help beginning teachers succeed.* Alexandria, VA: Association for Supervision and Curriculum Development.

Gray, W. A., & Gray, M. M. (1985). Synthesis of research on mentoring beginning teachers. *Educational Leadership, 43*(3), 37–38.

Gursky, D. (2000). Supply and demand: Finding and training the teachers we need for the 21st century. *On Campus, 20*(4), 10–12, 15.

Guskey, T. R. (2000). *Evaluating professional development.* Thousand Oaks, CA: Corwin Press.

Haberman, M. (1987). *Recruiting and selecting teachers for urban schools.* Reston, VA: Association of Teacher Educators and ERIC Clearinghouse on Urban Education.

Hardcastle, B. (1988). Spiritual connections: Proteges' reflections on significant mentorships. *Theory Into Practice, 27*, 201–208.

Harrington, T. (2001, July 19). Teacher learns tough lesson in first year. *Concord Transcript, The Contra Costa Times,* pp. 1, 5.

Heller, D. A. (2004). *Teachers wanted: Attracting and retaining good teachers.* Alexandria, VA: Association for Supervision and Curriculum Development.

Hoffman, J. V. (2004, January/February/March). Achieving the goal of a quality teacher of reading for every classroom: Divest, test, or invest? *Reading Research Quarterly, 39*(1), 119–128.

Huling-Austin, L. (1987). Teacher induction. In D. M. Brooks (Ed.), *Teacher induction: A new beginning.* Reston, VA: Association of Teachers and Educators.

Huling-Austin, L. (1988, April). *A synthesis of research on teacher induction programs and practices.* Paper presented at the annual meeting of the American Educational Research Association, New Orleans, LA. (ERIC Document Reproduction Service No. ED302546)

Huling-Austin, L. (1992). Research on learning to teach: Implications for teacher induction and mentoring programs. *Journal of Teacher Education, 43*, 173–180.

Hunter, M. (1994). *Enhancing teaching.* New York: Macmillan.

Ingersoll, R. (2001). Teacher turnover and teacher shortages: An organizational analysis. *American Educational Research Journal, 38*(3), 499–534.

International Reading Association. (2003). *Prepared to make a difference: Research evidence on how some of America's best college programs prepare teachers of reading.* Newark, DE: International Reading Association.

Interstate New Teacher Assessment and Support Consortium. (1992). *Model standards for beginning teacher licensing, assessment and development: A resource for state dialogue.* Washington, DC: INTASC. Retrieved February 4, 2007, from www.ccsso.org/content/pdfs/corestrd.pdf.

Johnson, S. M., Birkeland, S., Kardos, S. M., Kauffman, D., & Peske, H. G. (2001). Retaining the next generation of teachers: The importance of school-based support. *Harvard Education Letter, 17,* 6–8.

Jonson, K. (1997). *The new elementary teacher's handbook: (Almost) everything you need to know for your first years of teaching.* Thousand Oaks, CA: Corwin.

Jonson, K. (1998). Providing a safety net for new teachers: University-school district collaboration. *Academic Exchange Quarterly, 2*(2), 21–28.

Jonson, K. (1999a). Parents as partners: Building positive home-school relationships. *The Educational Forum, 63,* 121–126.

Jonson, K. (1999b). [Survey of 28 mentor-teachers in the San Francisco Unified School District]. Unpublished raw data.

Joyce, B., & Showers, B. (1982). The coaching of teaching. *Educational Leadership, 40*(1), 4–12.

Joyce, B., & Showers, B. (1983). *Power in staff development through research on training.* Alexandria, VA: Association for Supervision and Curriculum Development.

Joyce, B., & Showers, B. (1995). *Student achievement through staff development.* White Plains, NY: Longman.

Katz, L. (1972). Developmental stages of preschool teachers. *Elementary School Journal, 23*(1), 50–51.

Kay, R. S. (1990). Mentoring: Definition, principles, and applications. In T. M. Bey & C. T. Holmes (Eds.), *Mentoring: Developing successful new teachers.* Reston, VA: Association of Teacher Educators.

Knowles, M. S. (1980). *The modern practice of adult education: From pedagogy to andragogy.* River Grove, IL: Follett.

Kram, K. E. (1985). *Mentoring at work.* Glenview, IL: Scott Foresman.

Laczo-Kerr, L., & Berliner, D. (2002). The effectiveness of Teach for America and other under-certified teachers on student academic achievement: A case of harmful public policy. *Educational Policy Analysis Archives, 10*(37).

Levine, A. (1999, April 7). Dueling goals for education. *New York Times,* p. A21.

Levine, S. L. (1989). *Promoting adult growth in schools.* Needham Heights, MA: Allyn & Bacon.

Levinson, D. (1986). *Seasons of a man's life.* New York: Knopf.

Looking at Student Work. Retrieved October 6, 2006, from www.lasw.org.

Lortie, D. C. (1975). *Schoolteacher: A sociological study.* Chicago: University of Chicago Press.

Losing sleep. (2001, January 23). *Contra Costa Times,* sec. D.

Lou Harris & Associates. (1991). *The Metropolitan Life Survey of the American Teacher, 1991. The first year: New teachers' expectations and ideals.* New York: Author.

Mandel, S. (2006, March). What new teachers really need. *Educational leadership.* Alexandria, VA: Association for Supervision and Curriculum Development.

Marsick, V. J. (Ed.). (1987). *Learning in the workplace.* New York: Croom Helm.

Mathison, C. (1996). The challenges of beginning middle and secondary urban school teachers. *Issues in Teacher Education, 5*(1), 5–18.

McGreal, T. L. (1983). *Successful teacher evaluation.* Alexandria, VA: Association for Supervision and Curriculum Development.

Means, B. (2000). Technology in America's schools: Before and after Y2K. In R. S. Brandt (Ed.), *Education in a new era.* Alexandria, VA: Association for Supervision and Curriculum Development.

Mid-Continent Regional Educational Laboratory. (1983). *Time management.* Kansas City, MO: Author.

Moir, E. (1999). The stages of a teacher's first year. In M. Scherer (Ed.), *A better beginning: Supporting and mentoring new teachers.* Alexandria, VA: Association for Supervision and Curriculum Development.

Moir, E. The phases of first-year teaching. Santa Cruz New Teacher Center. Retrieved February 3, 2007, from www.newteachercenter.org/article2.php.

Moir, E. Putting new teachers at the center. Santa Cruz New Teacher Center. Retrieved September 21, 2006, from www.newteachercenter.org/article3.php.

Moir, E., & Gless, J. Quality induction: An investment in teachers. Santa Cruz New Teacher Center. Retrieved September 21, 2006, from www.newteachercenter .org/article1.php.

Moran, S. (1990). Schools and the beginning teacher. *Phi Delta Kappan, 72,* 210–213.

Murray, M. (1991). *Beyond the myths and magic of mentoring.* San Francisco: Jossey-Bass.

National Commission on Teaching and America's Future. (2003). No dream denied: A pledge to America's school children. Washington, DC.

NCTE ELL Task Force. (April 2006). *NCTE Position Paper on the Role of English Teachers in Educating English Language Learners (ELLs).* National Council of Teachers of English, Urbana, IL.

Odell, S. J. (1990). Support for new teachers. In T. M. Bey & C. T. Holmes (Eds.), *Mentoring: Developing successful new teachers* (pp. 3–23). Reston, VA: Association of Teacher Educators.

O'Neil, J. (1993). Supervision reappraised. *ASCD Update, 35*(6), 1, 3, 8.

Orlich, D. C. (1989). *Staff development: Enhancing human potential.* Boston: Allyn & Bacon.

Pearson, M. J., & Honig, B. (1992). Problems confronting beginning teachers. In *Success for beginning teachers: The California New Teacher Project* (pp. 5–14). Sacramento: California Department of Education, California Commission on Teacher Credentialing.

Portner, H. (1998). *Mentoring new teachers.* Thousand Oaks, CA: Corwin.

Portner, H. (2001). *Training mentors is not enough.* Thousand Oaks, CA: Corwin.

Portner, H. (2006). *Workshops that really work: The ABC's of designing and delivering sensational presentations.* Thousand Oaks, CA: Corwin Press.

President Clinton's Call to Action for American Education in the 21st Century. (1997). Retrieved February 8, 2002, from www.ed.gov/updates/PresEDPlan

Raspberry, W. (2000). Lessons teachers beg to be taught. *ATE Newsletter, 33*(4), 3.

Roche, G. R. (1979). Much ado about mentors. *Harvard Business Review, 57*(1), 14–16, 20, 24–27.

Rowley, J. B. (1999). The good mentor. *Educational Leadership, 56*(8), 20–22.

Ryan, K. (1986). *The induction of new teachers* (Phi Delta Kappa Fastback No. 237). Bloomington, IN: Phi Delta Kappa Educational Foundation.

Sacks, S. R., & Brady, P. (1985, March-April). *Who teaches the city's children? A study of New York City first year teachers.* Paper presented at the annual meeting of the American Educational Research Association, Chicago.

Santa Cruz New Teacher Center. Teacher induction. Retrieved December 30, 2006, from www.newteachercenter.org.

Scherer, M. (Ed.). (1999). *A better beginning.* Alexandria, VA: Association for Supervision and Curriculum Development.

Scherer, M. (2001). Making standards work. *Educational Leadership, 1*(1), 5.

Schlechty, P. C., & Vance, V. S. (1983). Recruitment, selection, and retention: The shape of the teaching force. *Elementary School Journal, 83,* 469–487.

Schmoker, M. (2006). *Results now: How we can achieve unprecedented improvements in teaching and learning.* Alexandria, VA: Association for Supervision and Curriculum Development.

Schultz, B. (1999). Combining mentoring and assessment in California. In M. Scherer (Ed.), *A better beginning: Supporting and mentoring new teachers.* Alexandria, VA: Association for Supervision and Curriculum Development.

Sergiovanni, T. J. (1992). Collegiality as a professional virtue. In *Moral leadership: Getting to the heart of school improvement.* San Francisco: Jossey-Bass

Shanker, A. (1995, February 22). *Sink or swim.* Retrieved February 8, 2002, from www.aft.org/stand/previous/1995/012295.html

Showers, B. (1985, April). Teachers coaching teachers. *Educational Leadership, 42*(7), 43–48.

Shulman, J. H., & Colbert, J. A. (Eds.). (1988). *The intern teacher casebook.* San Francisco: Far West Laboratory for Educational Research and Development.

Shulman, J. H., & Sato, M. (Eds.). (2006). *Mentoring teachers toward excellence: Supporting and developing highly qualified teachers.* San Francisco: Jossey-Bass.

Smith, R. D. (1993). Mentoring new teachers: Strategies, structures, and successes. *Teacher Education Quarterly, 20*(4), 5–18.

Stanulis, R. N., & Weaver, D. (1998). Teacher as mentor, teacher as learner: Lessons from a middle-school language arts teacher. *The Teacher Educator, 34*(2), 134–143.

Suárez-Orozco, C., & Suárez-Orozco, M. M. (2001). *Children of immigration.* Cambridge, MA: Harvard University.

Teacher voices: The beginning teacher project. (1996). *Newsletter of Beginning Teacher Induction Network, 1*(3), 3.

University of California Santa Cruz, Department of Education. (2003). Tips for new mentors. *Reflections, 6*(1), 15.

U.S. Department of Education. (1997). *Seven priorities of the U.S. Department of Education* (Working document). Retrieved February 8, 2002, from www.ed .gov/updates/7priorities

Varah, L. J., Theune, W. S., & Parker, L. (1986). Beginning teachers: Sink or swim? *Journal of Teacher Education, 37*(1), 30–33.

Wilson, S. M., Floden, R. E., & Ferrini-Mundy, J. (2001). *Teacher preparation research: Current knowledge, gaps, and recommendations.* Seattle: WA: Center for the Study of Teaching and Policy.

Wilson, B., Ireton, E., & Wood, J. (1997). Beginning teacher fears. *Education, 117,* 380, 396–400.

Wong, H. K., & Wong, R. T. (1991). *The first days of school: How to be an effective teacher.* Sunnyvale, CA: Harry K. Wong.

Zachary, L. J. (2000). *The mentor's guide: Facilitating effective learning relationships.* San Francisco, CA: Jossey-Bass.

Zey, M. G. (1984). *The mentor connection.* Homewood, IL: Dow Jones-Irwin.

Zimpher, N. L., & Grossman, J. E. (1992). Collegial support by teacher mentors and peer consultants. In C. D. Glickman (Ed.), *Supervision in transition: 1992 yearbook of the Association for Supervision and Curriculum Development* (pp. 141–154). Alexandria, VA: Association for Supervision and Curriculum Development.

Index

**CORWIN
PRESS**

The Corwin Press logo—a raven striding across an open book—represents the union of courage and learning. Corwin Press is committed to improving education for all learners by publishing books and other professional development resources for those serving the field of PreK–12 education. By providing practical, hands-on materials, Corwin Press continues to carry out the promise of its motto: **"Helping Educators Do Their Work Better."**